The Roman Wars in Spain:

The Military Confrontation with Guerrilla Warfare

The Roman Wars in Spain:

The Military Confrontation with Guerrilla Warfare

Daniel Varga

Pen & Sword
MILITARY

First published in 2015 by
Pen and Sword Military

An imprint of
Pen & Sword Books Ltd
47 Church Street
Barnsley
South Yorkshire
S70 2AS

ISBN 978 1 47382 781 3

A CIP catalogue record for this book is available from the British Library

Printed and bound in England
By CPI Group (UK) Ltd, Croydon, CR0 4YY

Pen & Sword Books Ltd incorporates the Imprints of Pen & Sword Aviation,
Pen & Sword Family History, Pen & Sword Maritime, Pen & Sword Military,
Pen & Sword Discovery, Pen & Sword Politics, Pen & Sword Atlas, Pen & Sword
Archaeology, Wharncliffe Local History, Wharncliffe True Crime, Wharncliffe
Transport, Pen & Sword Select, Pen & Sword Military Classics, Leo Cooper, The
Praetorian Press, Claymore Press, Remember When, Seaforth Publishing and
Frontline Publishing

For a complete list of Pen & Sword titles please contact
PEN & SWORD BOOKS LIMITED
47 Church Street, Barnsley, South Yorkshire, S70 2AS, England
E-mail: enquiries@pen-and-sword.co.uk
Website: www.pen-and-sword.co.uk

Contents

Acknowledgements

This book was made possible by the support and assistance of a number of people whom I would like to thank. I am deeply indebted to my lovely wife Raia, my children Barak, Michal and Arik, my parents for their devoted education and full support of my studies throughout the years. I would like to thank my supervisor, Prof. Lucien Poznanski, for his tight and practical guidance throughout my doctorate studies; my thanks to Prof. Yulia Ustinova and Prof. Steve Rosen for their support, attention and helpful comments.

To my directors Dr. Dov Nachlieli and Dr. Ygael Israel, thank you for your unreserved support, without which I would have not completed my doctorate and this book; I would also like to thank Ms. Shlomit Handelsman for the linguistic editing, Ms. Avital Sampson-Mofaz for the translation into English, Dr. Ianir Milevski for his devoted help in the proofreading of the text, and to all of my friends and colleagues. My thanks also to Juan Valdes Sierra director Museo de Caceres, Dr. David Bea Castaño and Prof. Fernando Quesada Sanz for kindly giving materials for this book.

List of Abbreviations

AEspA	Archivo Español de Arqueología
AJPh	American Journal of Philology
BAR	British Archaeological Reports
BSAA	Boletín del Seminario de Estudios de arte y Arqueología
Cl. Phil.	Classical Philology
Complutum	Publicaciones del Departamento de Historia de la Universidad Complutence
CuPUAM	Cuadernos de Prehistoria de la Universidad Autónoma de Madrid
Geríon	Revista de Historia Antigua
Gladius	Estudios Sobre Armas Antiguas, Armamento, Arte Militar y Cultura en Oriente y Occidente
Habis	Publicaciones de la Universidad de Sevilla, Arqueología, Filología Clásica
Hist.Ant	Historia Antigua
Hispaña	Revista Española de Historia
JRA	Journal of Roman Archaeology
JRMS	Journal of Roman Military Studies
JRES	Journal of Roman Equipment Studies
JRS	Journal of Roman Studies
Klio	Beitrage zur alten Geschichte
Latomus	Revue d'études latines
MB	Madrider Beitrage
MemHistAnt	Memorias de Historias Antiguas
OxFJA	Oxford Journal of Archaeology
Paleohispanica	Revista Sobre Lenguas y Culturas de la Hispania Antigua
PALLAS	Revue d'études antiques
ProcSocAntiqScot.	Proceedings of the Society of Antiquaries of Scotland
RPA	Revista Portuguesa de Arqueologia

Chapter One
Introduction

Guerrilla Warfare

Guerrilla is a word of Spanish origin, which means 'a small war'. Nowadays, we are witnesses of conflicts in which guerrilla warfare is used quite successfully: in Iraq and Afghanistan, especially against the American army and its allies.

The term 'guerrilla' is a modern term, originating in Spain of the nineteenth century, when it was used in the context of fighting the French occupying armies, led by Napoleon. However, we know that guerrilla warfare, as a phenomenon, already existed in different locations in the ancient world.

Gann indicates that there is a variety of warfare situations in which guerrilla tactics are used. These include fighting against an occupying force, fighting between different tribes, and small-scale and specific operations as part of a large-scale war, in parallel with a 'conventional' war. As early as the third century BC, the Chinese commander Sun-Tzu wrote about guerrilla warfare. The Hasmoneans used it against the Seleucid forces in the second century BC.

Though this is a well-known phenomenon, to date no extensive research has been conducted about the use of guerrilla warfare in conflicts that preceded the Second World War. On the other hand, a lot has been written about guerrilla warfare in the 1940s-1970s in Latin America, Asia and Africa.

This book is focused on the period during which the Roman Republic attempted to conquer the Iberian Peninsula (207-19 BC); the Roman army had to face an enemy that employed different combat methods, including some 'unconventional' ones ('guerrilla warfare').

Research Methods and Objectives

The book is based on two pillars: the first is history (literary sources and historical research), and the other is archaeological research. Archaeology is extremely important in understanding the techniques of the armies that took part in the Hispanic wars – both Roman and those of the local peoples, as well as their different components.

The ancient sources did not elaborate on military issues, either due to a lack of interest or as a result of a lack of understanding of this subject. Even sites of famous battles such as Cannae or Zama are not precisely identified.

The archaeological research published in the last two decades in Spain and Portugal complement the picture of the Hispanic wars. Battlefield Archaeology, which is a new area in archaeological research, used in Spain and Portugal, enables a high-resolution analysis of battlefield sites, which leads to more accurate conclusions. Since a battle is a one-time event, it produces a picture frozen in time, along with all its inherent advantages and disadvantages. This new area of research supplements the study of army camps, fortifications, and burial grounds in particular.

This work has three objectives. The first is to examine how the Roman army performed in terms of tactics and strategy, in the conquest of Hispania. This includes examining the changes that have taken place in the Roman army and all its different components, due to the constraints that arose during the wars (tactics, equipment, mobilization methods, etc.).

This requires a consideration of the numerous limitations and drawbacks that made matters worse for the Roman army, such as the enormous distance from the Apennine Peninsula, which caused considerable logistical issues, or dealing with an enemy that knows the terrain well, or the many limitations related to military mandates awarded to commanders according to the Roman Republic method, to name just a few.

The second objective is to examine the reasons – military, political, economic and others – why it took Rome almost two hundred years to conquer the entire Iberian Peninsula.

The third objective is to examine the changes that were introduced – following the wars and as a result thereof – to the Roman army in terms of its composition, organization and weapons; changes that emerged as a result of thinking and drawing conclusions, and not due to constraints in the field.

Sources and history of the research

The historical research of the Roman conquest of Hispania is based on the ancient sources we have today, which are all Greek and Roman. All these sources which are different in terms of preferences, interests and styles, describe the wars of Hispania from the Roman point of view. This viewpoint is based on stigmas and prejudices against peoples considered as barbarians and uncultured, by the Romans and Greeks. Therefore, these sources are one-sided and biased.

The first important source for the study of the Roman wars in Hispania is Appianus, who was born in Alexandria at the end of the first century AD. During the reign of the emperor Hadrianus, he was granted Roman citizenship, moved to Rome and established his permanent residence there. During the reign of the emperor Antoninus Pius, he became part of the imperial administration. The exact date of his death in unknown, but it is estimated c.161 AD.

Appianus tried to chronicle the history of the Roman State from its inception until his own time in his work *Roman History*, according to the wars it fought. Ten books are almost fully preserved from his work:

those which describe the Second Punic War, the wars in North Africa, Mithridates wars and the civil wars in the last days of the Roman Republic. Several sections survived from the books that describe the Roman wars that preceded the Second Punic War and the wars against the Hellenistic kingdoms. All the books describing the history of Rome beginning with the establishment of the empire were lost. The most ancient version of Appianus' work which we have today – which probably serves as the basis to all fifteen later versions – is the handwritten version from the eleventh century found in the Vatican Library, marked (V) Vatican, Vat. Gr. 141. This manuscript also includes a description of the wars against Hannibal and the wars in North Africa. Appianus gained very little recognition as an historian in itself, but due to the comprehensive scope of his work, he is considered as an historical source and as a means for discovering sources that preceded him.

The part which is of interest to us is the sixth book *Iberike*, in which he describes the Roman wars in Hispania from beginning to end, during the reign of Augustus.

The most important sources following Appianus are the works of Polybius and Titus Livius. Polybius was an Achaean who lived in Rome in the second century BC. He wrote about the Second Punic War in Hispania as well as the wars that the Romans have fought in Hispania following the Second Punic War. He is mostly renowned for his work *The Histories or The Rise of the Roman Empire*, which describes in great detail the events that took place in the Mediterranean Basin during the period of 220 to 146 BC. In this book, Polybius describes the war between Rome and the Carthaginians in Hispania, as part of the Second Punic War. Especially important are Polybius' accounts of the journey of his patron and hero, Scipio Aemilianus, in his war against the Celtiberian city of Numantia, in which he accompanied him as his assistant in the middle of the second century BC.

Livius lived at the time of Augustus, 59 BC to AD 17. He wrote a work about the history of Rome *Ab Urbe Condita Libri*, which is his major work and the only one that was preserved. It includes 142 'books' which cover the history of Rome since its legendary foundation until the death of N. Claudius Drusus in 9 BC. His work portrays Rome in depth, but unfortunately, only thirty-five books were left intact, and these are the ones covering Rome's history since its foundation until 293 BC, and the period of 219 to 167 BC. Only outlines or excerpts were left from the other books. Livius describes the wars in Hispania at length, though not at the length or thoroughness of Appianus. His style is literary and he is not personally involved in the events that he describes.

Several additional sources have assisted in some specific issues. Herodotus is an important source for the geography and population of Hispania, though he focuses in his writings mainly on the Phoenician and Greek colonies.

Strabo and Valerius Maximus serve as important sources of information about the peoples of Hispania. In addition, Strabo is a unique source for learning about Hispania, in the way it was regarded in the Ancient World. Strabo has also written about the climate and geography of this region, its natural resources and population. Diodorus Siculus and Silius Italicus have written about the different peoples of Hispania.

Julius Caesar mentions the peoples of Hispania – some his allies, others his rivals – in the *Gallic War* and in the chapter about the Hispanic wars in *De Bello Civico*. His book is based mainly on the works of Polybius.

The following works have provided information that assisted in solving the puzzle which is the subject of this book: Cicero's book *De Officiis* (On Duties), Valleius Paterculus' work *Compendium of Roman History*, and Lucius Annaeus Florus. Plutarchus has written about several personages, to whom a substantial portion of this book is dedicated, such as Tiberius Gracchus, Sertorius, Julius Caesar and Augustus. I have also used the works of Florus, Plinius Maior [Pliny the Elder], Suetonius *Lives of the Caesars*, and *Dio* Cassius' (Roman History), which have all added important information, especially to the last chapter discussing the Roman conquest of Hispania and the Cantabrian and Asturian wars commanded by Augustus and Agrippa.

To date, the research of the Roman conquest of the Iberian Peninsula was characterized by an almost total disconnection between historical and archaeological research. The historical research of the Roman wars in Hispania was pushed aside to a secondary priority, as opposed to research of wars that have taken place at that time in the east. The heritage and glorification of Alexander the Great – not only in the Hellenistic world – have attracted the attention of researchers who have studied (and still are studying) the history of the confrontation between Rome and the Hellenistic kingdoms, rather than the wars of Rome in the west, especially during the second century.

In addition, the little historical research about Roman wars in Hispania was conducted, as seen further on, by researchers whose main language was neither Spanish nor Portuguese. Most of these researches are over 20 years old and do not refer at all to the abundance of the archaeological findings, which were, and still are, being discovered in excavations in Spain and Portugal in recent decades. These excavations shed new light on the Roman conquest in the regions, which are now Spain and Portugal, and are managed by researchers from these countries, and so, most of their findings are published in their own language. Most of the articles that discuss the findings of the archaeological excavations include the researchers' reference to the ancient sources, but not to the current historical research.

It can be said that the research conducted in Spain and Portugal regarding the Roman army, concerning army camps and military equipment is less advanced in comparison to research conducted in other countries, where there are remains of the Roman conquest. In addition, until a few decades ago, only a few Roman army camps have been excavated in the Iberian Peninsula, and for fewer yet were the findings published. It should be noted that in the Iberian Peninsula there are more remnants of Roman army camps from the time of the Republic than in any other place that was under the control of the Empire. Therefore, it can be concluded that the lack of interest stems from biased thinking and that the activities of the Roman army in 'some remote corner of the world' waged against 'barbarians' is probably not interesting enough when compared to the confrontation that took place at the same time in the East between the great Roman army and the Hellenistic kingdoms, characterized by sophistication and reputation.

The researchers who did continue, nonetheless, to explore and study the Roman army camps dating to the time of the Republic, have probably done so due to the fact that the Roman wars for the conquest of Hispania lasted a very long time (218 to 19). Furthermore, the most impressive and numerous remnants of the Roman army camps from the period of the Republic have been found in the Iberian Peninsula.

The pioneer in the research of the Roman army in Spain was Adolf Schulten, who excavated the camps of Cornelius Scipio and the siege wall around the city of Numantia. He has also excavated additional army camps, including several camps of Nobilior. Schulten has used the romantic approach in his research, and has come to look for a 'Heroic Numantia' that had fought against the 'cruel Roman conqueror', equipped with Appianus' book describing the Numantine wars. Schulten was determined to confirm – or to refute – these descriptions using excavations and topographic research.

Despite that, and in spite of the many erroneous interpretations, Schulten is the father of Roman archaeology in Spain. Nowadays, Spanish archaeologists have begun excavating and publishing listings of classical Spanish antiquities. M. Gomez Moreno has conducted a preservation survey of monuments of Roman Hispania, and J. Ramon Melida has excavated in Roman sites that were of interest to him, especially in Numantia and Merida. Research of the Roman army in Spain was discontinued at the beginning of the 1930s until the end of the 1940s, due to the Spanish Civil War and the Second World War.

Since the Second World War, Franco's Spain was isolated from Europe. The wish to reconnect the country to the western heritage has led to the research of classical Spain in general, and the period of the Roman Republic in particular. Antonio Garcia Bellido and his students have renewed this research, particularly the study of the Roman army camps from the period of the Roman conquest of Hispania. Bellido, an archaeologist and historian, has succeeded in interpreting ancient texts in a new way, and adding new layers to modern historical research. Bellido's research centred around the different peoples that inhabited the Iberian Peninsula, their social, economic and material culture, as well as the relationships between the different Iberian peoples and the Phoenicians, Carthaginians and Greeks.

The last decades of the twentieth century produced many studies dealing with the Iberian Pennisula in the Roman period, some of which refer to the Roman conquest itself. The process of the assimilation of the Roman culture by the different conquered peoples was also studied, as well as the impact of the conquest on life in these regions from different aspects. Curchin has written about the assimilation of the Roman culture by the local peoples during the conquest, as well as the influence of these peoples on the Roman conquerors. Other researchers such as Bosch, Knapp, and Keay have written about Roman Hispania. Alarcão has written about the history of Roman Lusitania, present-day Portugal, at that time.

Several studies were written about the peoples that inhabited the Iberian Peninsula on the eve of the Roman arrival at the end of the third century BC, out of which the following books can be mentioned: Lorrio's book discussing the Celtiberian peoples, and Monet and Quesada's book dealing with the wars in the Celtiberian world, from the sixth century until Scipio Aemilianus. Many researchers, including Adcock, Brunt, Goldsworthy, Harmand, Keppie, Parker, Peddie, Simkins and Smith have studied the Roman Republican army and its place in the Roman world.

This is a good place to commend the book by Roth about the logistics of the Roman army. This book discusses the topic while examining all the complexities and difficulties associated with engaging in remote wars in the ancient era. Different issues dealing with the Roman armies in conquering Hispania were studied by many researchers including Astin, who wrote about the Roman governors of Hispania Ulterior; Blazquez has written about the influence that the conquest of Hispania had on Rome, Cerdan focused on the Roman army's contribution to the urban development in the north-western part of the Iberian Peninsula; Curchin has studied the assimilation of the Roman culture within the Iberian Peninsula following the conquests; Knapp has dealt with different issues regarding the conquest of Hispania, whereas Quesada has studied the warfare in the Celtiberian world.

Quesada is the leading Spanish archaeology researcher of the Roman army, Lusitanians, Celts and Iberians in the Peninsula. He has written the leading articles on these topics in the last decade, among which the ones that should be pointed out are the articles about weapons, and especially about the Spanish *gladius* and its origin. He has also written about other weapons that were used by the Hispanic peoples, and the Hellenistic and Carthaginian influences on these weapons, and about fighting techniques in Hispania. Most of his writings are based on archaeological findings.

Morales and Morillo have written about the remnants of Roman army camps related to the conquest of Hispania; Richardson has studied the Roman government in the different Roman provinces of Hispania; Trevino has written an overview of the activities of the Roman armies in Hispania; Corzo Sanchez and Millar have written several articles about different issues in the Second Punic War in Baetica, and their influences on the future development of the province.

The roots of the archaeological research regarding the Roman Republican army in Spain are found in the works of A. Schulten from the beginning of the twentieth century. As previously mentioned, he has dealt with army camps, especially Scipio's siege camps in Numantia. He was particularly interested in finding parallels between the findings of the excavation and Polybius' description of the camps. As of the 1990s, a renewed research is underway regarding Schulten's findings, especially concerning the siege walls and camps around Numantia. The new excavations discovered, for example, that the camps that Schulten 'populated' with entire legions, were in fact secondary camps; it was also discovered that the camp in La Raza was built after Scipio's time, contrary to Schulten's opinion; the ceramic and numismatic findings in the new excavations in Gran Atalaya-Renieblas have changed the dating of the site; it turned out that the ancient layers of the camp, that had previously been dated to the period of Sertorius, belong in effect to the period of the campaign of Scipio Aemilianus.

In recent years, new research has been conducted on Roman weapons. The excavations in Osuna and the renewed excavations in Numantia (Caceres El Vieo) are extremely important. Additional archaeological research includes that of Morillo, who studies the Roman army camps, especially those of the seventh legion 'Gemina', and the third 'Macedonica'. Additional studies published about this subject include: Cerdan, Morales, Quesada, and other researchers, most of which are based on the latter. The new excavations in the 1990s have shed new light on Roman weapons from the second century, on which information was only partial. I have already mentioned Quesada's article where he has described how the Spanish *gladius* has become the standard weapon of the Roman legionnaire in the second century. His research is based on archaeological remains, but it also uses many literary sources. In 1990, Connolly also published an article about the main Roman weapons during the period of the Republic. Most of the article is based on the new excavations that have taken place all over Spain.

In recent years, there is a renewed interest in the study of Roman army camps from the period of the Republic. In 2006, Angel Morillo and Joaquin Aurrecoechea edited a collection of articles named *The Roman Army in Hispania* in preparation for the 20th International Roman Frontiers Congress. This book examines the status of the research of the Roman army in Spain and Portugal from different aspects, especially the archaeological one.

In general, the tendency in current research relating to the Roman conquest of Hispania is to update old research that was conducted at the beginning of the twentieth century until the 1940s. At present, many historical studies, mostly archaeological, and mostly by Spanish researchers, are underway, as mentioned previously.

The Geography of Hispania

There has been no other region in the Roman Empire where the relationship between the geographic-topographic conditions and the political-military issue has been as strong as in the Iberian Peninsula. Therefore, it is essential to know the complex geographic context in order to understand the military actions of the Roman army in the region; actions that took place for over 200 years in the Iberian Peninsula, from the end of the Second Punic War in the year 216 BC in that region, until the complete conquest of Hispania by Augustus and Agrippa in the year 19 BC.

Some 80 per cent of the Iberian Peninsula's borders are maritime, while the rest borders the Pyrenees, which separate the Peninsula from the rest of Europe, rather than connecting between them. Most of the area is inhabitable, but the living conditions are harsh. This is due to the fact that most of the terrain is covered by high mountain ranges, forests and plateaus where the soil is thin and infertile. One exception is the southern fertile area, which also enjoys a very pleasant climate.

As stated, the terrain in the peninsula is mountainous. Spain and Portugal are considered among the most mountainous countries in Europe following Switzerland. The average altitude in Spain is over 600m above sea level. The highest mountain peaks are mostly in the Pyrenees, which stretch between the Mediterranean and the Cantabrian Sea, separating Spain and France: Pico de Anto – 3,375m, Monte Perdido – 3,355m, Cilindro 3,328m and Perdiguero – 3,321m. Additional high peaks are found in the Sierra Nevada mountain range in the south-west of Spain: Mulhacen Mountain – 3,478m (the highest mountain in the Iberian Peninsula) and Alcazaba Mountain – 3,392m.

Inland there is a plateau called Meseta Central which literally means the central plateau, at the height of 600-760m above sea level. The plateau is surrounded by mountain ranges, some of which stretch out into the Meseta. The western slopes of the plateau are moderately slanting towards Portugal and some rivers flow from it and constitute part of the border between Spain and Portugal. The Sistema Central mountain range (literally: the central system) crosses through the Meseta Central, and is described as the backbone of the plateau. This range divides the plateau into two parts: the northern and southern.

The northern part of the plateau is higher than the southern part and is smaller in size. The Sistema Central mountain range surrounds the capital city of Madrid. The mountains to the north of the city reach the height of 2,400m, while to the south, they are lower. The highest peak in the range, Pico Almanzor, is located west of Madrid and reaches the height of 2,600m above sea level. The summits of this range are covered with snow most of the year. Although the mountain range crosses the plateau, it does not constitute a barrier between the north and south. There are several passages which allow a relatively convenient passage of people and goods.

On the southern part of the Meseta range there are two mountain ranges: Montes de Toledo stretching to the east and Sierra De Guadalupe Mountains stretching to the west. The highest peaks of the two ranges reach 1,500m above sea level and more. There are many passages between the mountain ranges, including passages that connect the Meseta plateau to the Andalusia plains. The Tajo (Tagus) flows to the north of the mountain ranges, and separates between them and the Sistema Central mountain range.

The central plateau, the Meseta, is surrounded by mountain ranges including Sierra Morena to the south, Cordillera Cantabrica to the north, and the Sistema Iberico to the east.

The Sierra Morena and the mountains to the south of the plateau join the extensions of the Sistema Iberico in the east; to the west, they stretch to the north of the Valley of the Guadalquivir and join the mountains of South Portugal. The Valley of the river Guadiana separates these mountains and the Sistema Central mountain range. The mountains here are not very high and the elevation of their summit does not exceed 1,300m above sea level.

The Cordillera Cantábrica Mountains are made of limestone and stretch along the northern coast near the Bay of Biscay. The range is 182km long, and its peaks Picos de Europa are over 2,500m high. The Sistema Iberica Mountains join the Cordillera Cantábrica mountain range and stretch to the south-east as far as the Mediterranean. The total area of the Sistema Iberica Mountain range is 21,000sqkm. The height of the mountains in the north is above 2,000m and the highest peak is over 2,300m at the source of the Rio Duero.

Two mountain ranges that are not part of the Meseta plateau are the Pyrenees at the north-east and the Sistema Penibetico in the southeast. The Pyrenees stretch from the end of Cordillera Cantábrica mountain range as far as the Mediterranean. They create a natural border between Spain, France and Andorra. This is an actual barrier that has isolated Spain from Europe for entire periods of time in history. The crossing of the Pyrenees is done in the western and eastern ends. The passage in the centre is extremely hard. The mountain peaks are over 3,000m in some places, and the highest peak, Pico de Anto, rises above 3,400m. The Sistema Penibetico Mountains stretch from the southernmost point of Spain northward. The mountains stretch in parallel to the coast and reach the south of the Sistema Iberico. The Mulhacen Mountain rises south of Granada, in Sierra Nevada, which is part of the Sistema Iberico. This range includes additional peaks of over 3,000m above sea level.

The main plains in the Iberian Peninsula are the coastal plains, the Andalusia plain in the southwest of the country, which the river Guadalquivir runs through its centre, and the plain of the river Ebro in the northeast of Spain. The width of the Spanish Mediterranean coasts ranges from 20km to just 1km.

The Andalusia plain is in fact the wide banks of the Guadalquivir. The river widens in the direction of the estuary and reaches its maximum width in the Bahia de Cadiz. The Andalusia plain borders the Sierra Morena range in the north and the Sistema Penibetico Mountains in the south.

The valley of the river Ebro consists of the Ebro plain and the mountain slopes surrounding it from its three sides: the Sistema Iberico from the south and west, and the Pyrenees from the north and east.

Although there are over 180 rivers and streams in Spain, only one river, the river Tajo (Tagus: Tejo in Portuguese) reaches the length of 1,000km. Only ninety rivers stretch over 96km. All others are shorter and some are seasonal streams, which sometimes dry up completely. Most rivers get their waters from the mountains that border the Meseta Central, and most flow westwards, across Portugal and empty into the Atlantic Ocean. One exception is the Ebro, whose stream bed flows east, and it empties into the Mediterranean. One of the most important rivers in Spain is the Guadalquivir, 657km long. This river serves as a water source for a fertile agricultural area. In addition, it is the only river in the peninsula that is used for sailing, and the Seville port that lies on its banks is the only inland port in Spain, from which it is possible to sail to the ocean. All other rivers in the peninsula are very hard to sail on. Other important rivers are the Miño (Minho) in the northwest, and the Duero (Douro) and Guadiana in the south.

The Iberian Peninsula is located in a region of temperate climate, but is characterized by different climates in the different areas, due to the changing terrain and landscape. There are three different climate types: continental, marine and Mediterranean.

Continental climate, which characterizes most of Spain, prevails in the centre of the peninsula. It is dominant in the central Meseta plateau, the mountains stretching from the plateau eastward and southward and in the Ebro plain. The summer is hot and dry, the winter is cold, the temperatures are unstable and the rain is scarce.

A marine climate prevails in the north of the peninsula. The winter is relatively cold and the summer temperature is hot but not blazing. The harsh climate and the infertile land in the area have made it, according to Strabo, desolate and unappealing.

Mediterranean climate prevails in the Andalusia plain and the southern and eastern coasts. The temperatures are comfortable most of the year, and rain falls irregularly, especially in the autumn and winter.

In terms of precipitation, Iberia can be divided into two areas. The first is the north which includes the Basque Country, Cantabria, Asturias and Galicia (north of Portugal). This is the 'Rainy Spain', the area of the marine climate. It rains here most of the year, but less in the summer. The annual rainfall reaches 650mm. The size of 'Rainy Spain' is about one third of the country.

The other area is the southern part, from the Cantabrian Range southwards, and is called 'Dry Spain'. The climate in this region is partly continental and partly Mediterranean. Rain is irregular and in changing quantities and the weather is pleasant most of the year.

Throughout history, the mountain ranges have constituted a significant obstacle for passage and travel in the Peninsula. There were, obviously, routes that crossed the mountains such as the route from Terraco to Ilerda through the Ebro valley; the route which crossed the mountains, from Saguntum on the coast to Jalon Valley; the route from Cartagena to the Baetiz area through the Genil Valley, and so on.

None of these routes offered an easy passage, so it is probable that most travel and passage in the period of Ancient Roman was done via the coast, from the Pyrenees in the north to Cartagena in the South of the Peninsula.

These geographic and topographic conditions have played an important role in the creation of a wide variety of peoples and cultures in the Iberian Peninsula, from the prehistoric period until our time.

Peoples of Hispania during the third century

Many peoples have inhabited the Iberian Peninsula on the eve of the Roman arrival, at the end of the third century. These are the peoples the Roman army eventually confronted on its long journey to conquer all of Hispania.

The inland tribes were mostly of 'western' Indo-European origin: the Celts and Iberians. Greeks and Phoenicians-Carthaginians inhabited the Mediterranean coast. Greeks inhabited mainly the eastern coast and the Phoenicians-Carthaginians lived in the southern coast.

Celts and Iberians

The 'native' peoples did not leave behind many written sources apart from several inscriptions and some graffiti. Therefore, the research of these peoples depends entirely on external sources – Roman and Greek – and the archaeological findings.

In recent years in Spain, there is a renewed interest in the Roman period, which has led in turn to the study of these peoples. Some of these studies, most of which are archaeological, are conducted on behalf of municipal authorities, which have 'local-patriotic' motives, which may create a biased picture.

The ancient sources contain quite a lot of references to the pre-Roman Hispanic peoples. These references express prejudices of Greeks and Romans towards these peoples, ranging from mere contempt to actual hostility. Therefore, these should not be taken at face value. The interest of the Greek and Roman writers (Polybius, Livius, Pliny, Strabo, Appianus and others), has increased once the Romans have entered Hispania. If information regarding the situation

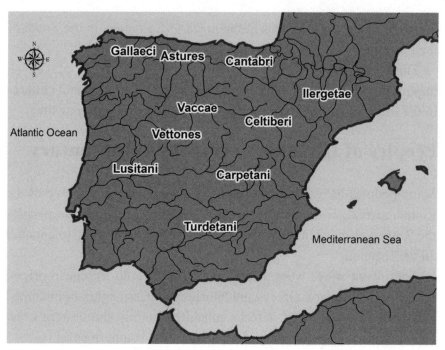

The major ethnic groups.

in Hispania prior to the Second Punic War is scarce, then the amount of information provided by other sources increases from the end of the third century onwards.

Livius writes of Hannibal's speech before his soldiers prior to the war they were about to fight in the centre and north of Hispania. In this speech, Hannibal allegedly described central Hispania. This speech is probably fictitious, but it is important because it illustrates the common image of central and western Hispania in the first century: a wild, poor and sparsely populated region. Livius claims that the population in these regions was involved mainly in sheep herding. One may wonder whether this saying is the outcome of the negative attitude of the Romans towards shepherds, who are considered 'barbarians'.

The sources did not distinguish between the different peoples. Pliny the Elder states there were forty-five peoples who lived in Hispania. Each had its own culture, customs and leaders. Only from the second half of the second century onwards did the first signs of 'Iberian' identity emerged, characterized by relatively uniform cultural characteristics, as a result of the battles against the Phoenicians and especially the Romans. Aennius Florus wrote that the Hispanic peoples hadnever wanted to fight against Rome, nor build an empire, nor even to unite against a common enemy. The Hispanic people discovered their own strength as they had resisted the Roman army continuously for 200 years; from 218 BC when Gnaeus Cornelius crossed the Pyrenees until the year 19 BC in the reign of the first *imperator* Augustus. During this time Hispania was classified as a military zone until the time of Emperor Domitianus at the end of Roman habitation on the Iberian Peninsula around the first century AD.

Strabo, who wrote in the first century AD at the time of the Emperor Tiberius, indicates that the Greeks knowledge was very limited, while the Romans lacked interest in the subject. The third book of his work *Geographica* is the most important source of information about the peoples of pre-Roman Hispania. He described these peoples as weak, divided tribes who had fought each other constantly and were therefore unable to unite against a common enemy such as the Romans.

In a legend that came to us through Parthenius of Nicaea (the Greek poet of the first century), the mythological fathers of the Hispanic peoples, Iberus and Celtus, appear as the sons of Heracles and the nymph Astrope, daughter of Atlas.

The peoples that inhabited Hispania on the eve of the Roman arrival, can be placed in terms of geography and topography, and characterized in terms of ethnicity and politics. However, the attempt to accurately position the different tribes is not crowned with success.

And yet, the 'native' inhabitants of the Peninsula can be divided into three groups: the first inhabited the hills in the north and west of *Mesetas* (Hispania) and consisted of semi-nomad peoples.

Due to the geographic-topographic barrier of the Pyrenees, these tribes lived far away from the influence of the Mediterranean peoples (Phoenicians and Greeks). And therefore, the assimilation of the Roman culture would be the longest and hardest in comparison to the other Hispanic peoples. It is possible that unlike Livius' statement, the economy of these tribes was not based on sheep herding, but rather it complemented their income, if they even did it for a living at all. It is more than likely that they conducted business with the urban centres in the south and east, and not just raided them. Most of them were of Celtic origin and spoke an Indo-European language that survived at least until the second century AD. Certain tribes are known to us by the Roman names given to them: Gallaeci, Cantabri and Astures. These tribes were divided into smaller tribes whose living area were usually quite small, and included a fortified village on top of a hill and the area around it. This matches the Celtic social structure. The structure was preserved to a large extent, probably due to the topographic barriers of mountains and forests, which prevented the establishment of tighter social ties with other peoples and the adoption of social alternatives. Silius Italicus has written that the Cantabri, a northern tribe, were a strong people who could endure harsh climate conditions and lack of food. He added that the Cantabri considered old age as a period of weakness and sickness, and therefore preferred to die a sudden death at the height of their prime, and better yet, in battle.

The second group includes the peoples known to us by the general name of Celtiberians and Lusitani. These peoples, who were at the centre of opposition to the Roman conquest during the second century, have transformed in time to the origin of the identity of the two nations that have eventually divided the Iberian peninsula between them; Spain's Celt-Iberians and Portugal's Lusitani.

The term 'Celt-Iberians' describes a population of a non-uniform origin, which consists of different populations that have merged over time. This is, at least, what Diodorus Siculus and Appianus have suggested. To them, the Celtiberians were Celts who had merged with the Iberians. In recent years, there have been several attempts to divide the history of the Celtiberians into sub-periods. The most popular division is Lorrio's, into four periods from the eighth until the first century. This division is based on the differences in the material culture as was discovered in tomb excavation. Lorrio named the period between the third and first centuries the Late Celtiberian period.

The Lusitani were a federation of 300 tribes that inhabited the north-centre and west of the Peninsula. We are not certain about the

Lusitanian political structure. Alarcão, the Portuguese researcher, has divided them according to their geographic location: Lancienses, Tangi and Palanti.

The Celtiberian social structure consisted of three circles. The inner circle was the nuclear family, which the Romans recognized as *Gentilitatus*. This is a society whose sons are blood-related and have a mutual ancestor. They share the same religion and have joint ownership over their living area.

The second circle was wider. The Romans recognized it as *gens*, and it consisted of several nuclear families. Several 'Genses' created a rather stable federation, which is parallel to a tribe.

Two bodies probably ran the Celtiberian tribes: an assembly of the people which was open to all adults, and a council of the tribal chiefs or town elders. In addition, there was the 'sole leader' who ruled in collaboration with the council of elders (or tribal chiefs). The authority of this leader is not clear, but the Roman sources identified him as the king. Florus claimed that the main reason for the fierce resistance of the Lusitanians and Numantians to the Romans was that only they, out of all the tribes, had true leaders; but he might have referred to the human quality of their leaders, so his words should not be understood literally.

The social-economic structure of these tribes was not uniform. The Vaccei for example, were the northernmost tribes. They lived in relatively large autonomous communities, but they were dependent upon a tribal capital city, fortified on top of a hill. When fighting against the Romans, they used to gather the tribe members and livestock into the city walls and entrench themselves within the walled city. The Arevaci were semi-nomads and herded sheep for a living. Only during the first century did the Romans succeed in forcing them to live in permanent settlements, following a process of assimilation of Roman culture.

The Celtiberians lived in small, widely-spaced villages and in a number of small, but well fortified cities, such as Numantia and Tramentina. Recent calculations, based on the size of the Celtiberian villages and number of tombs dug over the years, estimate the size of the Celtiberian population as at least 250,000 people, and even up to 450,000 inhabitants. The latter estimate is the more popular one.

The Celtiberians and Lusitanians were the most militant peoples in the Iberian Peninsula, and those who caused the most casualties to the Roman armies (Rankin 1996). We have quite a lot of evidence from different sources regarding the character of the Celtiberians, which undoubtedly quote from earlier sources. Strabo, Valerius Maximus and Livius describe them as a militant, courageous and very inquisitive people. In addition, it is told that they volunteered for gladiator fights, and that their objective in battle was victory at all costs. Returning home safely after being defeated in battle or returning alive after their leader had lost his life in battle was considered disgraceful. They also opposed the burning of bodies, because they believed that the soul rose to the heaven after the vultures had fed off the corpse.

Diodorus of Sicily has written that among Celtiberians were those who believed that the gods would bestow favours on those who treated strangers well. A graphic anecdote told by Strabo and Diodorus of Sicily says that the Celtiberians used to brush their teeth with horse urine. Silius Italicus said that the women were socially active, and that they performed all the jobs that men considered degrading, including planting and harvesting the fields.

There is very little information about the religion of the Celtiberians. Strabo wrote that they worshipped primitive, non-anthropomorphic gods. No evidence of druids or priests of any kind was found in Hispania.

During the first and second centuries, the Celtiberian social structure underwent many changes, resulting from the encounter with the Romans. The emphasis shifted from the public to the private domain; new social and economic classes evolved, particularly of people with no assets or income that chose to serve as mercenaries for the rich, or join the Roman army auxiliaries.

The third group includes the population of the coast and the south. The tendency in the first Spanish studies dating from the nineteenth century until the middle of the twentieth was to idealize the Iberian society prior to their encounter with the Romans, like the idealization of the Gauls during their war against Julius Caesar. They were described as industrious, freedom-loving people, who were 'spoiled' by their encounter with the Romans and the Roman conquest. New research – though not comprehensive enough – indicates that the facts are far more complicated. This research also clearly indicates that the changes in society and culture began centuries before, as a result of the ties with the Greek cities, and even more with the Phoenicians and Carthaginians.

The Iberians were peoples of a more urban nature than the Celts. They are known in the world of research as 'Iberians' though their exact origin is unknown. In addition, it is unknown to what extent they had merged with the Celts, or what language they spoke, but it was probably not an Indo-European language. In the few inscriptions and graffiti discovered and dated to the period between the fifth and second century, it is possible to distinguish at least two different languages, with an alphabet of probably twenty-eight letters, which was greatly influenced by the Phoenician language.

The archaeological evidence indicates the existence of small villages, located in high, easily defensible locations. The exceptions were the rich, relatively large settlements. Carmona and El Carambolo, for example, display the architectural influence of the Greek cities. Maybe they were even founded by the Greeks and at some point, merged with the Iberian population, being assimilated into the local culture. The Iberian city of Ulastret, near Emporion, was excavated rather intensively. An ancient scattered village was uncovered there, dating to the beginning of the seventh century. A collection of hand-made pottery was discovered, in which clear Phoenician influence is apparent. The later settlement was a relatively large fortified city, dating to the period between the sixth century and roughly the year 200. This settlement had a Greek style of design, the streets were a Hippodamian grid and the buildings were rectangular. Fifty per cent of the ceramic collections found were Greek or of a Greek character and they probably originated from nearby Emporion. An acropolis was built in the upper part of the city but it was damaged in the Middle Ages and has not been excavated to date.

The dominant type of settlement model in the Iberian world was shaped like a pyramid: a fortified settlement built on top of the hill (*atalaya*), small villages connected by routes were located in the centre of the slope, and the fields were below. It seems that the agricultural units that surrounded the cities and villages constituted the basis for the Iberian economy.

In recent years, excavations have begun in more Iberian sites. These have uncovered large buildings that included a big hall (probably for hosting and reception of delegations), warehouses, a central patio, probably of some ritual role, and the remnants of a top floor, probably living quarters. The purpose of these buildings is still debated.

In Andalusia alone, more than 6,000 bronze god statuettes and 800 clay statuettes were discovered. This far exceeds the number of statuettes found in all the 'ritual' buildings excavated so far, put together. It is unclear whether these were palaces or shrines, or maybe, as many believe, palace-sanctuaries, i.e. a structure of political, administrative and ritual purposes all together.

The structure of the Iberian society was stratified and the power was in the hands of the kings and local nobility. The Iberian nobility merged into the Phoenician and Carthaginian nobility through arranged marriages based on interests. On the one hand, these marriages were intended to bring the conquerors closer to the local peoples, and on the other, they enabled the local nobility to get closer to positions of power and hold key roles in the controlling Phoenician-Carthaginian administration. It should be pointed out that there is a controversy among researchers regarding the existence of an 'Iberian culture' as such. A few researchers, consider the Iberians as groups of Celtic tribes that inhabited the Iberian Peninsula, and were later influenced by the Greeks, but mostly by the Phoenicains. They established cities or settled in Phoenician or Greek cities along the Mediterrenean coast and in the rich and fertile southern area, present-day Andalusia.

In summary, it can be said that despite significant differences between the geographic units, the Hispanic peoples that inhabited the different regions of the peninsula had enjoyed a substantial political and cultural progress, on the eve of the Roman arrival. Some researchers, such as Sopenia, claim that the resistance to the Roman conquest was in fact the trigger to the union of the Celtiberians, and the element that shaped their culture.

The encounter of these peoples with Phoenician and Greek traders and settlers, or 'colonists', expedited the development of a relatively complex society led by a political elite, which attempted to model itself on the Phoenician elite but, in parallel, tried also to preserve ingredients from its original culture. This dominant class advanced the urban development on different levels and regions, along with the growth of an even more developed and complex society, which was eventually destined to be assimilated into the Roman-universal cultural world.

The Greeks

According to Herodotus, the first Greeks were colonists from Phocea that arrived on the Iberian shores at the city of Tartessus. They formed ties of friendship with King Arganthonius, who invited them to settle in his kingdom. This is, in fact, the beginning of the Greek settlement in Iberia.

The first Greek artefacts to be discovered in the Iberian Peninsula were found in the Huelva area. A limited number of pottery collections, especially kraters, were uncovered there, dating to the eighth century. The Greek pottery constitutes a tiny portion of the ceramic collection, which is much smaller than the Phoenician complex. No Greek pottery dated to the period between the middle of the sixth century and the end of the fifth, was discovered. Presumably, the reasons for this are found in the east, and maybe the sequence of wars there; the Persian Wars and The Peloponnesian War had an impact on the trade with the west. Around the year 400, pottery of a Greek nature emerged again, but this was, in fact, local Iberian pottery, especially from the kingdom of Tartessus, that had undergone a process of 'Hellenization', together with the rest of the components of the Iberian culture.

The first Greek colony in the peninsula was Rhodas. The settlers probably originated from the Isle of Rhodes, but some researchers think that their homeland was the Greek colony of Massilia (Marseille). Emporion was founded south of Rhodas, which is present-day Emporia.

Strabo mentioned two more colonies south of Emporion: Alonis and
Akra Leuke (Alicante), which the Romans called Lucentum. Strabo
even mentioned several Greek colonies on the southern edge of
Hispania, in the valley of the river Guadalquivir, which no longer
existed in the third century; they were probably destroyed by the
Phoenicians or Carthagenians. Despite these statements, we have
no irrefutable evidence – neither archaeological nor historical – that
the Greeks did settle on the Mediterranean coast of Hispania prior
to the sixth century. We need to differentiate between two types of
Greek settlements. The first includes colonies established by settlers
originating from true Greek cities or by people of old Greek colonies
from across the Mediterranean, such as Massilia. These cities were
founded mainly in the north-eastern coast of Hispania, present-day
Cataluña; e.g. Emporion and Rhodas. These cities were built on the
basis of the Greek Hippodamian grid, and included all the buildings
that were found in the homeland cities. In addition, as opposed to other
Greek and Phoenician cities, coins were minted in these cities, which
is a clear sign of independence.

A second type of settlement comprises those which are alternatively
considered by the sources as either Greek or Carthaginian.
Archaeological excavations in these settlements have uncovered
numerous remains of buildings, coins and pottery of Greek origin, or
of a Greek nature. It is possible that, at the time of their establishment,
these were Greek colonies at some point, but that control was seized
by a foreign power, either Carthaginian or Iberian; or maybe they had
never been Greek, but were influenced by Greek cities and adopted
many Greek cultural characteristics.

Emporion was the richest city in the region, and had quite a
substantial influence over the nearby Greek and Iberian cities and
villages. Archaeological excavations in the city have uncovered pottery
collections that had been imported over time from the east – especially
Greece and Asia Minor – which are found in all the layer sequences in
the city. In addition, they have found lots of pottery originating from
artisan workshops in Emporion and the Iberian villages surrounding
the city and further away.

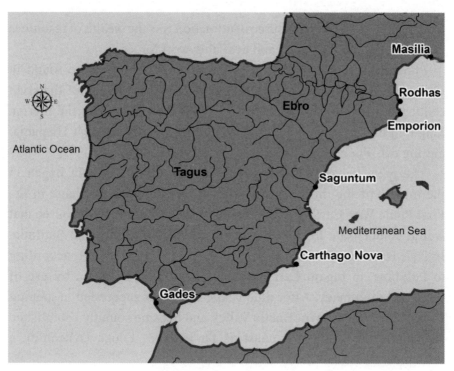

Phoenician and Greek major colonies.

Phoenicians and Carthaginians

The common approach today is that Gadis (Cádiz) was the first Phoenician colony founded in the south of Hispania at the beginning of the eleventh century. A structure dating to the beginning of the tenth century, which was identified as a temple to the main Phoenician god, Melqart, reinforces this claim. It was probably the Kingdom of Tyre that had founded Gadis and turned it into the bridgehead of commercial expansion on the southern coast of the Iberian Peninsula and the region of Baetica.

The first wave of Phoenician settlement in the south of Spain had already begun in the seventh century. Though the Iberian Peninsula is located in the western end of the Mediterranean, the Phoenicians had no difficulty sailing over there, since they had colonies and trading stations in Sicily and Sardinia. Hispania represented a new and profitable market, especially for Phoenician goods, and there was hardly any competition from the Greeks. Another source of attraction was the wealth of resources in the region, such as metal and available workforces.

Phoenician remnants dating to the seventh century were found in Gadis, Abedera and Malaka (Malaga). As early as the end of the sixth century, Carthage – an ex-colony of Tyre – had taken over the Iberian kingdom of Tartessus, which led to control over south-east Hispania, cutting off 'Phoenician' Hispania from Tyre.

The great wave of Carthaginian settlement in Hispania began in the middle of the third century, after Rome defeated Carthage in the First Punic War. Carthage was forced to seek an alternative source that would compensate for the loss of its colonies in Sicily and Sardinia. In 237, Hamilcar Barca was sent to Hispania. He was sent, according to Polybius, to regain Carthaginian control over Hispania by use of force and diplomacy. After nine years, Hamilcar succeeded in gaining control over the affluent Baetis Valley and became soundly established also along the south-east coast as far as Akra Leuka (Alicante), a settlement that he founded and fortified.

Hasdrubal, Hamilcar's nephew, carried on the Carthaginian conquests following the death of his uncle, using similar methods as his predecessor. Diodorus Siculus says that Hasdrubal married the daughter of the Iberian king and was proclaimed the commander of all Iberians. In the year 228, Hasdrubal founded the city of Carthage, known to Romans as Carthago Nova, present-day Cartagena. He fortified the city, and built a big port and a magnificent palace, which became the centre of control of the Barka family in Hispania. Hannibal, the son of Hasdrubal, expanded the Carthaginian-controlled area as far as the river Ebro.

The main characteristics of the Roman army at the end of the third century

The Roman army that arrived in Hispania with Scipio at the beginning of the Second Punic War was an army designed for seasonal wars in the Apennine Peninsula and the islands surrounding it. The legions were drafted for short wars close to home and were released at the

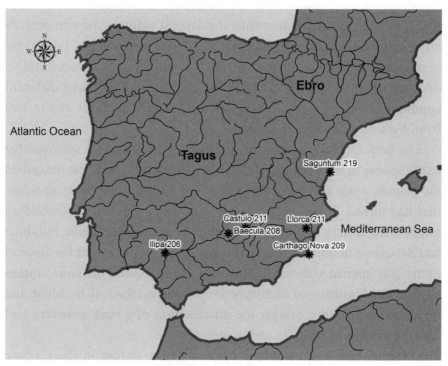

Major battles of the Second Punic War.

end of the war, several months later. This was about to fundamentally change (see below in chapters 4 and 5, discussing the legion and its components: the changes in the number and nature of the warriors, changes in the sub-units, the development of logistics, changes in the weapon collections and standardization), especially due to the Hispanic Wars.

In the third century, once Rome had seized control of the Apennine Peninsula and turned itself into the most powerful city in the region, it began the process of becoming a major power throughout the Mediterranean basin. The main rival standing in the way of the Roman Republic in realizing this objective was Carthage, the undisputed ruler in the western and central Mediterranean waters.

Rome had fought on several fronts simultaneously: in the west against Carthage and in the east against the Hellenistic kingdoms and league of Greek cities. But it was the First and Second Punic Wars that had transformed Rome into the largest military power, and its army had evolved from medium-sized into the best and most powerful of the time, and for centuries to come. Nonetheless, it had turned into a dynamic organization that was flexible and able to fight under different conditions, and even adopt weapons and warfare methods and tactics from both its allies and enemies.

The first detailed account of the Roman army and its methods for battle appear in the writings of Polybius. In his sixth book, he described the Roman army and its components, and called it the 'war machine' that had turned Rome, according to him, from a power of secondary importance in Italy into the ruler of the Mediterranean Basin. Polybius had described in great detail the Roman army on the eve of the Second Punic War against Hannibal (221-202). He discussed the conscription process for legions and auxiliary forces, the method of building and organization of army camps, the introduction of a rank structure and also the system of benefits and punishments.

Polybius had written in the context of the defeat in the Cannae battle and the recovery following this battle. But his objective was to glorify the Republican method. This method allowed the Romans to organize shortly after a defeat that seemed final, mobilize another army, defeat the Carthaginians and become the masters of that world. It should be pointed out here that Polybius had written decades after the end of the war, and so not all of his descriptions can be accepted as relevant to the period that he wrote about. Furthermore, it is likely that he described the Roman army of his time – the middle of the second century; an army that he had personally fought against as a cavalry officer.

Certainly the Roman army described by Polybius is actually the army of Scipio Aemilianus, which Polybius accompanied during the Numantine War. He had witnessed how an army that was defeated several times by the armies of the Hispanic tribes, worked diligently and trained feverishly under the leadership of Aemilianus, and underwent a thorough rehabilitation process. The army of Aemilianus had taken initiative in the war and won the first siege battle that took place in Hispania. Also the greatest of them all: the siege of Numantia, which served as the centre of resistance to the Roman domination in Hispania. This is in fact, the ideal army described by Polybius in his sixth book; the army of his hero and patron.

An example of this is found in the Roman army camp excavated in Renieblas, near Numantia. Layer Number 3 was dated to the middle of the second century and precedes the Numantine War by more than twenty years. Therefore, I think that there is no reason for surprise due to the differences – which are not that many – between this camp, and that described by Polybius in the sixth book.

The legion was the main part of the Roman army, operating as an autonomous unit, a type of small-scale army. It is unclear when the legion had become the basic unit of the Roman army, but it is possible that this occurred at the beginning of the fourth century, in works by Livius and Plutarchus. They both attribute the change undergone by the Roman army and the transition from the phalanx to the manipular legion (consists of *manipules*) to the reforms introduced and legislated by Marcus Furius Camillus in 386, following the Roman defeat by the Gauls.

In the third century, the Roman army became the army of the citizens: the consuls used to conscript civilians for specific military campaigns. The army consisted of four legions, which included 300 horsemen in each. In periods of peace – which were quite rare – four legions were recruited, two of which were commanded by the two consuls. In the case where additional forces were recruited, *praetors* or other senior magistrates would command them.

The 'on alert' legions received identification numbers from one to four. They did not have the chance to form their own tradition; the number of warriors was not fixed nor was the composition, due to the fact that they were recruited for a limited period of time and for a specific objective.

Army service was, as stated, a right reserved for citizens, but only to those who were owners of property and other possessions. This was for two reasons: first, the recruits had to purchase their own equipment, and not all citizens could afford that. The second was that a property owner risked the chance of losing his property in the event of a defeat, and so this was considered a good incentive for him to fight more fiercely than a person who had nothing to lose. The citizens with no *capite censi* (property) were recruited in times of emergency and equipped by the State. In the second century, the minimal property required for approval to serve in the Roman army was worth 400 Greek drachmas.

This conscription policy was put to the test during the Numantine War in the 30s of the second century. Like the period of the end of the third century during the wars against Hannibal, the human and economic resources of Rome were stretched almost to the limit. A severe shortage of manpower throughout the military, from ordinary soldiers up to senior officers, had forced the Romans to be less selective in their rules for conscription; moreover, the terror that the war had spurred in Rome, also led to a compromise regarding the men recruited. This was, in fact, the beginning of a long period, at the end of which all Roman citizens were required to serve in the army.

The age of conscription was 17, and the service period was limited to a maximum of sixteen years. At the age of 46, citizens were allowed to be exempt from military service. However, this was somewhat flexible and depended on operational requirements. As we see further on, the length of military service had been extended in the second and first centuries.

The composition and size of a legion varied and was based on the duties for which it was recruited. The standard number of soldiers in a legion ranged from 4,200 to a maximum of 6,000; the number of horsemen attached to each legion ranged from 200 to 300. A basic legion also included 4,200 warriors. The infantry was composed of 1,200 'light' soldiers, swordsmen with leaders for each group, and 600 veterans. A legion was divided into thirty *manipuli*, which constituted two *centuriae*. The senior centurion was the commander of all *manipuli*. In battle formation, this centurion was stationed in *manipule* the furthest to the right. The swordsmen, leaders and veterans were divided into ten *manipuli*, numbered from one to ten.

The legion was based, as stated above, on infantry soldiers. These soldiers were classified according to designated duties, and each duty required dedicated equipment. The younger and less wealthy soldiers served as *velites* (light infantry). The light infantry also included the *antesignani* (intermediate force). However, the might of the legion was the 'heavy' infantry, which was divided into three main units: the *hastati, principes* (swordsmen) and *triari* (veterans).

Polybius tells in his writings that all *hastati* carried two *pilum* (heavy spears), one heavier than the other. And indeed, different types of *pila* spears were found in archaeological excavations carried out at Renieblas siege camps in Numantia. These spears were dated to the period of the Numantine War, which had taken place in the 30s of the second century. The *pilum* had a 60cm iron shank joined to a 1.3m wooden shaft and was some 2m in length.

The *hastati* were usually young warriors, and this unit was positioned in battle in the front row of the legion formation. The second unit was considered as the elite, and was positioned in the second row of a battle formation. The third unit consisted of *antesignani*, who were positioned in the third row of the battle formation or completely behind the lines, and served as the camp guards during the battles.

The *velites* were equipped with a *hastae velitariae* (light spear), a sword and a helmet. The *triari* was also equipped with a spear and carried a body shield. The *principes* and the *triari* were equipped with a helmet, body armour, a sword and a *scutum* (wide shield).

It has already been mentioned that the legionnaries positioned in the first two rows of the formation carried heavy spears. However, in the last decades of the second century, and the first century in particular, the differences between the various units were blurred to a large extent, in terms of weapons, and the entire legion began using the same weapons. Sumner uses the term 'institutional fossilization' when trying to explain the phenomenon of using names with seemingly no relation to the object. He relates this to the preservation of ancient names for objects, positions, etc., in spite of the many changes that the names, roles or way of action have undergone. This is apparent in particular in the names of the units of the Roman legion in Polybius' version from the second century. The *hastati* used the *pilum* and not the *hastae*, and the name of the unit was probably a trace from an ancient period – possibly the fifth century – in which the Roman army was organized according to the Macedonian phalanx formation, and

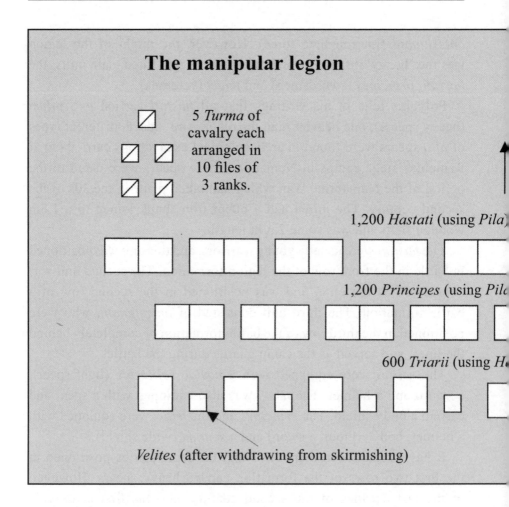

The manipular legion

5 *Turma* of cavalry each arranged in 10 files of 3 ranks.

1,200 *Hastati* (using *Pila*)

1,200 *Principes* (using *Pila*)

600 *Triarii* (using *Ha...*)

Velites (after withdrawing from skirmishing)

the *hastati* did use the *hastae*. The *principes* were positioned in the second row of the battle formation and not in the first, as their name implies (the main ones, or first and foremost). If we continue the same line of thought, thean it is likely that in earlier time, the *principes* were indeed positioned in the first row of the battle formation. This is also relevant to the *triari*. These warriors were known as *pilani*, carriers of the *pilum*, but their main weapon was the *hastae*.

The manipular legion[1]

The legionnaire's main weapon was a medium size, double-edged sword, which would be replaced by the famous Spanish sword, used by

5 *Turma* of cavalry each arranged in 10 files of 3 ranks.

:ntury 20 files and 3 ranks

:entury 20 files and 3 ranks

10 files and 6 ranks

Celtiberian warriors in the Hispanic Wars of the second century. It should be mentioned that archaeological excavations have uncovered several samples of *gladius* from the time of the Republic, and these were longer than those of the *principate*. The *gladius* was a cutting and stabbing weapon which was used by legionairies and also auxiliary forces.

The legion would enter battle in a formation that consisted of three rows of combat infantry soldiers. The battle tactics was usually very clear and simple: head-on assault in a formation. First to fight were the swordsmen; they threw the spear then attacked with a drawn sword. In case the attack failed, the leaders would provide backup in order to hold back the enemy. The veterans would enter the battle, as a last resort, if the army faced the threat of defeat.

Each legion had its own small *alae equites* (cavalry wing) that included between 200 and 300 horsemen, commanded by an officer, a *praefectus equitum*. The cavalry was divided into *decuriae* (units of ten), each commanded by a *decurio*. Three *decuriae* formed a *turma* of thirty-two *equites alaris* (horsemen), who operated under the command of the senior *decurio*. Each legion included ten *turmas*. The main duties of the Roman cavalry were: raiding the enemy, reconnaissance, and providing backup to the legion formation in battle and pursuit of a retreating enemy.

The Romans were not considered to be exceptional horsemen, and the cavalry unit was the weakest part of the army. Therefore, they would recruit warriors from their allies to serve in the cavalry. It was possible to join as a single horseman or as complete auxiliary unit. Horsemen were recruited from around the Roman world, especially North Africa and Germany. Almost all of the soldiers in these units were foreign, and the units were called *alae* (wing), since they were positioned on the sides of the battle formation.

The legion was commanded by six *tribuni militum* (military tribunes) of the senator class. Some of the tribunes were elected in the *tribuni comitati* (tribunes' council) and others were chosen by the senators. The officer echelon was not selected from ordinary civilians; they could only expect to reach the rank of centurion. The centurions were chosen by tribunes from among the veterans and bravest soldiers. When commanding the different *manipuli*, a centurion was given the title of *hastatus prior* (senior swordsman), *principes prior* (senior leader) and *pilus prior* (senior spear bearer).

As I have mentioned at the beginning of this chapter, and will continue to describe and explain in chapters 4 and 5, this entire formation was about to change during the conquest of Hispania. The army led by Agrippa which had been cheered for its victory in the Hispanic Wars at the end of the first century, was completely different from the army of the Scipios that fought at the end of the third century.

Chapter Two
The Roman Wars in Hispania

Hispania's importance to Rome in the third century BCE

The available sources do not contain any evidence whatsoever of Roman interest in Hispania, prior to the fall of the city of Saguntum to the Carthaginians. The only references include an observation concerning the Barca family gaining power, as well as a comment regarding the preservation of the treaties between Rome and Hasdrubal; also between Rome and Saguntum. This is an undisputed fact in the world of research.

Although the Romans had fought many wars in the peninsula during the course of the first half of the second century, the entire Hispanic issue was overshadowed by the wars fought in the Hellenistic east. These wars against barbaric bands of *latrones* (robbers) were quite different from those fought against Philip V or Perseus of Macedon, or Antiochus III the Great, ruler of the Seleucid Empire, both in terms of the glory bestowed upon the warriors, and of the potential for financial gain. While the wars in Hispania were as dangerous as those in the east, only in the middle of that century, when the Numantine and Lusitanian wars broke out simultaneously, did the Romans reluctantly turn their attention to Hispania.

In the year 218, on the eve of the Second Punic War, Hispania was mostly under Carthaginian rule, and that is why the Roman Senate was an interested party. Polybius claimed that the main reason for the Second Punic War was the Carthaginian conquest of Hispania, which provided the Carthaginians with a staging post for an attack on Rome. It also enabled them to have access to financial resources and excellent manpower. Presumably, the decision by Rome to declare war on Hannibal was made due to the votes of the 'conservative' side in the Roman Senate. This side had imposed very harsh conditions on Carthage at the end of the First Punic War, and urged the conquest of Sardinia and Corsica, although there was no provocation from either country. This same side considered the Carthaginian conquest of Hispania as a pretext for another war.

Some researchers believe that the plans for the conquest of Hispania and the destruction of Carthage were in existence from the outset. They claim that the Roman Senate, or at least its conservative side, had provoked the Carthaginians by sending delegates to Hamilcar Barca with an offer to divide Hispania along the route of the river Ebro: the area north of the river would be ceeded to Rome, and that south of the river to Carthage. This offer was sent in the hope that it would be rejected by the Carthaginian leader.

The next step of the provocation was to interfere with internal affairs of Saguntum, a city located on the Mediterranean coast, to the south of the Ebro. Although it was on the 'Carthaginian side', the city had 'special' relations with Rome; but no defence treaty.[2] Rome used the *amicitia* (friendship) with Saguntum as a justification to declare war on Carthage, so that it could be considered as a *bellum iustum* (a just war).

It should be mentioned that not all citizens of Saguntum were aligned with Rome. In the city there was a camp, the size of which is unknown, containing supporters of Carthage. Occupying Saguntum had enabled Rome to establish a bridgehead in Hispania, and confine Hannibal's army to the region for a significant time. Rome required time in order to recruit sufficient warriors to attack Hannibal; another army recruited by a consul was to attack the city of Carthage from Sicily. It is possible that the Romans believed that it would be extremely hard for Hannibal to conquer a well-fortified city as they had experienced during the First Punic War against Lilibaeum and Trepanum in Sicily.

The Romans probably thought that this would make Hannibal lose his enthusiasm to go on fighting and would draw back from continuing with his plans for conquest. This theory seems too convenient, because it assumes that the Roman Senate had known in advance about Hannibal's plans to invade Italy; but we do know that the Romans were actually surprised by this move. In addition, it is difficult to answer the question as to whether Hannibal himself, when rising to power, had known what he was about to do. In the end, all Roman plans to transfer military forces to Saguntum at an earlier stage – if we assume that there had been such plans – were cancelled when Gaelic tribes began launching extensive raids on Roman colonies in northern Italy which confined most of the Roman military units stationed in those regions for several years (222 to 226). Once Rome had declared war on Carthage, under the pretext that the city of Saguntum had been besieged by Hannibal's army, the Senate awarded an *imperium* (power of authority) over all of Hispania to the consul Publius Scipio. It is quite possible that Scipio was not at all pleased to be awarded authority over a seemingly unappealing province, located on the shore of the Mediterranean, and one that it would probably be hard – if not impossible – to conquer from the Carthaginians. His selection is proof that the Roman Senate had already considered, at that time, Hispania as a central theatre in the impending war. There are also clues that indicate that Rome had plans to rule Hispania directly once the war ended. The transfer of Roman forces to Hispania was delayed by the raids on colonies in northern Italy, and especially due to the fast movement of Hannibal and his army.

When Publius Scipio arrived at the river Rhône in the south of Gaul, Hannibal had already crossed the Pyrenees on his way to northern Italy. In spite of that, P. Scipio had moved a large portion of his army to Hispania, under the command of his brother Cnaeus Scipio who was given the status of *consul legatus*. This title probably indicates that C. Scipio had received the *imperium* directly from his brother, since P. Scipio was unable to get to the area, and there was no time to seek the approval of the Senate in Rome. Later during the war, the Senate itself used this method of appointment by awarding commanders in the field the *imperium pro praetore* (praetor authority), in order to make the chain of command more flexible and efficient during this very long war. Throughout the war, even when Hannibal threatened the city of Rome, the Senate continued to regard Hispania as a crucial region for the success of their overall war effort, and therefore diverted most of their forces over to the region.[3] Hispania was crucial to the success of Hannibal's campaign in Italy, because he had expected military reinforcements and finance, especially from the revenue from silver mines, that he needed in order to pay his (mostly mercenaries) soldiers. The Senate was aware that keeping Hannibal from his power base in Hispania would eventually lead to containing him in Italy and then destroying his army. Until the First Punic War, Rome had minted only a small number of gold and silver coins. At the end of the Second Punic War, the amount of Roman coins, especially gold, had increased dramatically as a result of exploiting the mines in Hispania. It is possible that many Roman Senators knew of the numerous silver and gold mines and wanted them for the Republic and also for their own benefit. In due course, the mines became the property of the State, which awarded contracts for their operation only to those close to power. Polybius writes that around the year 140, the silver mines of Carthago Nova alone provided revenue of 25,000 dinars a day. Moreover, the exploitation of these mines had greatly influenced the way Romans had conducted their wars. The copper mines were also of great importance to the Roman economy, as they were the source of high-quality material used for minting bronze coinage throughout the Roman Empire for centuries: at least from the second until the third century AD. Researchers disagree about the importance of Scipio's victories, but not regarding his successful organizational actions taken in the areas conquered from the Carthaginians. Scipio independently began a rapid reorganization of the political structure in Hispania, so that it would be completed before the end of his tenure. Most of his endeavours were invested in diplomatic actions – a Sisyphean work that led to treaties with the different local tribes.

Scipio Africanus in Hispania: Carthaginian Hispania moves to Roman control

The Romans were aware of local warriors, who fought as mercenaries, during their first battles with the Carthaginian army, and also in action against the armies of local Carthaginian allies. These encounters had already taken place in the war between Rome and Carthage, after the Romans had signed initial agreements with local tribes for different reasons. As we see later on, the constant shortage of Roman manpower, which has existed almost throughout the period of the Hispanic wars, had led Roman leaders in the field to numerous attempts to reach diplomatic solutions. It is quite possible that the shortage of manpower was one of the main reasons why the wars in Hispania lasted 190 years, and caused the loss of so many Roman lives.

On the eve of the Second Punic War, vast areas of the Iberian Peninsula were under the direct or indirect control of Carthage (in fact, under the control of the powerful Barca family). These regions included the south and south-central regions of the peninsula, and the coastal region, from the southern coast of present-day Portugal almost to the Ebro Delta in Tarragona, Spain.

When Hannibal Barca layed siege to the city of Saguntum, Rome declared war on Carthage. The prevailing view in the Senate was that the war would take place in Hispania and North Africa. As the main source of economic resources and manpower for Carthage, the Iberian Peninsula had become the central theatre in the war, second only to the Apennine Peninsula. A victory by Rome in Iberia was supposed to reduce, significantly, the status of Carthage as an equal opponent of Rome in the race for control of the west and centre regions of the Mediterranean Basin.

The Roman conquest of Hispania began in autumn 218, when Cnaeus Scipio crossed the Pyrenees with the consular army of his brother Publius Scipio, who had appointed him a *pro-praetor*. His army consisted of two legions that included cavalry units of Roman citizens, 14,000 infantry soldiers and 1,600 horsemen. Scipio based his strategy on two principles: speed and cooperation with the different tribes. C. Scipio had taken control of the port of Emporion, on the north-east coast of Hispania, by using diplomacy and force. He then advanced south-westwards to Terraco, an Iberian city, and established an army camp on high ground. Archaeological finds indicate that twenty years later, in Cato's period, the Iberian city of Oppidum had become a fortified Iberian-Roman *civitas* (city). Terraco would soon become the main port in Hispania for the Roman fleet, and also a military base for operations throughout the war in Hispania. Hasdrubal, a brother of Hannibal, who commanded Carthaginian forces responded quickly by making several raids on Roman forces, before retreating to his winter camp south of the river Ebro.

At the beginning of the summer of 217, C. Scipio sent his fleet of thirty-five ships along the Mediterranean to the area north of Ebro to intercept forty ships sent by Hasdrubal. Polybius and Livius indicate that the Greek city of Massilia participated in this battle with two 'spy ships' alongside the Roman fleet which achieved a crushing victory in the subsequent battle. It is probable that, according to Polybius, surveillance of the coast by the Carthaginians did not provide sufficient early warning of the approaching Roman fleet, as De Souza indicates. This success had led to two immediate results: the establishment of Roman supremacy in the north-west Mediterranean region and the Senate's decision to take advantage of C. Scipio's success and send his brother P. Scipio ,accompanied by large reinforcement force of thirty ships with 8,000 soldiers and war supplies, to Hispania.

P. Scipio arrived in Hispania, took command of the entire army and marched with his brother south along the coast to Saguntum, which was under Carthaginian control. The army layed siege to the city which then surrendered, after a short period, probably with the help from within the city of a Roman supporter who opposed the Carthaginians.

Hasdrubal had planned at the end of 216 or in early 215, to attack the Romans, but his orders from Carthage were to go to Italy to provide reinforcement to his brother Hannibal. In a battle on banks of the Ebro, Hasdrubal's army was crushed by the Romans and his orders cancelled.

The war had advanced and the Romans soon suffered shortages of supplies, money and manpower. Appeals to the Senate requesting assistance were not successful. According to Livius, the Senate was busy with more important and urgent problems than the needs of the Scipio brothers in Hispania: the fear of opening another front in Macedonia, the defeat in the battle for Lake Trasimeno, and probably the rift with Sicily. All these had reduced Rome's resources considerably. In spite of the events, the Senate did consider the war in Hispania important, and money was raised from 'public' companies based on the principle of loans in return for 'exemption' from military service. This was a desperate and dubious action taken to finance the supplies required for the fighting to continue.

The writings of Livius and Appianus do not contain clear information regarding the events in the war between the years 212 and 215. Livius does tell of the excellent leadership and successful journeys of the Scipios throughout Hispania up to Baetica in the south, but the accuracy of the description is questionable, due to the fact that the Romans did not succeed in conquering the whole of Saguntum until 212, and so, it is difficult to assume that they would dare move south without securing control of the eastern coast. Either way in the year 212 the entire east coast, from Emporion to Saguntum, was probably under Roman control and the supply route between Hispania and Hannibal (in Italy) was severed. It is possible that the Scipio brothers had already begun dividing the area between them in the same year. This is what Livius says, and Appianus implies this by writing that the Scipio brothers spent the winter of 212 in separate camps some distance from each other.[4] The two provinces had probably emerged in that year.

Livius had referred to Hispania in the plural, and mentioned that one was awarded to Publius and the other to Cnaeus Scipio. This indicates that they both had *imperiums*, they both headed a province, and formally, at least, they were equal. In 211, the brothers headed south and southwest to fight a deciding battle and win the war. P. Scipio commanded two-thirds of the Roman forces in Hispania and confronted the army of Hasdrubal and Mago, son of Gisco. C. Scopio had taken the remaining one-third, together with Celtiberian mercenaries, and confronted Hasdrubal Barca.

The two military operations ended with a Roman defeat, and written about by both Livius and Polybius, but their versions of events differ. According to Livius, the Celtiberians had betrayed C. Scipio and changed sides to Hasdrubal Barca's camp. According to Appianus, this act of treason did not take place at all. Either way, C. Scipio was forced to retreat and was killed while trying to contact his brother, after being defeated in battle. His brother, Publius, was killed earlier, when his army's attempt to outflank and prevent the Carthaginians from receiving reinforcements was thwarted.

A larger disaster was prevented thanks to the resourcefulness of *legate* Fonteius, deputy to P. Scipio, who rescued the remnants of the two brothers' armies. L. Marcius had received command of the army and successfully retreated to the northern coastal plain, which remained under Roman control.

It seems that this was the only region left under Roman control following the defeat Scipio armies. Marcius became a hero of legendary status in late Roman historiography: after all, he prevented Hannibal from receiving reinforcements for quite a long time.

This episode, the first in a long line of events on the road to the Roman conquest of Hispania, is an example of the difficulties that the Senate had to face when engaged in a war being fought a long way from Rome. This, in fact, is the first time that the Roman armies had fought so far away from Italy. It seems that battle tactics, and the strategy of the war in Hispania were determined by the Scipio brothers and not by the Senate. A problem that required an immediate solution could occur at any moment. Apart from awarding P. Scipio an *imperium* in 218, and to his brother C. Scipio in 212, the Senate was only responsible for the issue of supplies, though it is unclear to what extent. The Senate did not interfere with the decisions made by the Scipios, because even if they had tried, it would probably not have been practical.

In spite of L. Marcius' success, some senators were not pleased with the fact that he had been chosen by the soldiers in the field and received an *imperium*, without the formal approval of the Senate. It seems that he had taken the liberty to assume the authority of a *pro-praetor*; he had signed thus on a letter sent to the Senate describing the situation in Hispania. The Senate immediately began looking for a 'worthy' replacement for the Scipios and found him in C. Claudius Nero, who commanded an army at that time in the city of Capua, south of Rome, as a *pro-praetor*. Nero was sent to Hispania with a Roman army of 6,000 infantry and 300 horsemen, and a similar force from allies. His tenure in Hispania was short, and little is known of his actions.

Less than a year later, Nero was replaced by Publius Cornelius Scipio, the son of Publius Scipio. The reasons for replacing Nero are unknown; a lack of information regarding events in the years 212 to 211 eliminates the possibility that a disaster had occurred on the Roman side, and reinforces the argument that there had been internal political reasons which caused this replacement. It is possible that family ties, which had nothing to do with the war in Hispania, were behind this appointment.

The young C. Scipio was awarded *imperium pro consule* (consular authority) at the age of 25, without first holding the position of a consul. M. Iunius Silanus was appointed a *pro-praetor* in an inferior *imperium* than C. Scipio and was sent to Hispania to assist him in his mission. The Senate had probably hoped that he would supervise the actions of the young Cornelius Scipio.

In 210, Scipio and Silanus disembarked at the port of Emporion. The situation was stable, and it seemed that nothing had changed during Nero's tenure. The areas north of the river Ebro were still under Roman control. When Scipio arrived in Terraco he thanked the army for its courage in battle, especially to Marcius for his success in holding the territory even after the defeat of Publius and Cnaeus Scipio.

At the beginning of 209, C. Scipio launched a revolutionary operation; instead of splitting his forces and simultaneously confronting the three Carthaginian armies, commanded by Hasdrubal Barca, Hasdrubal son of Gisco, and Mago, he crossed the Ebro with 35,000 infantry, 2,500 horsemen supplemented by 5,000 soldiers from allies and rapidly advanced to Cartago Nova, the capital of the Carthaginian Hispania. Polybius and Livius claim that he reached the city in only seven days.

Scipio conquered the city in a lightning assault using two tactical moves: a frontal attack on the city's main gate, and simultaneously crossing the lake from the north. Mago, the garrison commander had no choice other than to surrender. By one move, Scipio had shifted the war into the heart of enemy territory; from then on he was the instigator and the Carthaginians were the defenders.

Following this victory, Scipio enjoyed greater prestige in the eyes of the Hispanic people, and many entered Terraco asking to join his army. These included Indibilis and Mandonius, the leaders of the Ilergetes, which were a powerful and important people of the Ebro valley area. Scipio granted their request and presented them with an Ilergetes prisoner that he freed from the Carthaginians. The Ilergetes swore allegiance to Scipio, and according to Polybius, they even wanted to call him 'king'. However, the title which originated from the period when Etruscan kings ruled Rome was unacceptable to Scipio and he declined.

Laelius travelled to Rome to inform of the conquest of Carthago Nova. On his return to Terraco, he carried a message from the Senate who were concerned at the reinforcements that Hasdrubal was to provide to Hannibal. These concerns may have dictated the course of the war.

On the other hand, Hasdrubal desperately needed a victory on the battlefield in order to halt the numbers of local men deserting from his army to the army Scipio.

The two camps began preparing for a general war, and probably for a large battle that would determine the outcome of the entire war. The battle finally took place at Baecula in the Baetiz Valley. Excavations run by the Andalusian Centre for Iberian Archaeology have found a battle site that matches descriptions, in terms of topography, by Polybius and Livius. Findings at the site, which include Carthaginian coins and buttons, weapons and pottery typical of that period, support identification.

Scipio managed to outflank Hasdrubal and win the battle, but the Carthaginian general escaped north with a large portion of his forces intact. Scipio did not chase Hasdrubal and only sent some of his forces to the Pyrenees. It is unclear what Scipio had hoped to achieve, but it is not possible that these forces alone would have prevented Hasdrubal from crossing the Pyrenees towards Italy. It is possible that these forces did join other forces commanded by Silanus.

Silanus was probably in charge of the area south of Terraco, and his mission was to prevent any possible Carthaginian movement to the north, in case Scipio had failed in the south. Following the battle at Baecula, the number of local leaders who swore allegiance to Scipio had increased; one-by-one they hailed and praised him as the king.

Scipio rejected the accolades and asked to be regarded merely as a supreme commander.

At the end of 208 and beginning of 207, the two sides were busy improving their positions. Livius mentions a meeting between the three Carthaginian commanders. After Hasdrubal Barca had left for the Apennine Peninsula, the command of the remaining Carthaginian forces was handed over to Hasdrubal son of Gisco, who retreated with them to the territories still loyal to Carthage. However, Mago sailed to the Balearic Islands in order to recruit new forces.

Later, Hanno a new Carthaginian commander arrived in Hispania and he joined Mago in creating a new army. Scipio sent Silanus to fight against them with 10,000 infantry and 500 horsemen, approximately half of his forces in Hispania.

In a battle at Sierra Morena, north of the Baetiz Valley, the Romans defeated the Carthaginians. Mago managed to escape with some 500 horsemen and used the remaining forces to strengthen the settlements under his control in the Baetiz Valley, thus preventing a final Punic defeat. Hanno was captured and sent to Rome with other prisoners. A Roman army commanded by Lucius Scipio, brother of Cornelius, enjoyed several successes but did not achieve the long-awaited victory. At the end of the military operation, L. Scipio was sent back to Rome to report on the progress of the war.

The final and largest battle of the war, the battle of Ilipa took place probably at the beginning of 206. The commonly-known location of the site (according to Polybius and Strabo) is in the village of Alcala del Rio, 13km north of present-day Seville, on the north bank of the river Guadalquivir in the Baetiz area. Strabo positioned Ilipa as 'close to the Baetiz River'. On the contrary, Livius and Appianus call the battle by different names, and therefore the identity of the site and its location are not at all certain.[5] One thing is certain: this was an 'all or nothing' battle. The forces of Mago and Hasdrubal son of Gisco were larger than those of Scipio. Polybius reports that the Carthaginians had 70,000 infantry and 4,000 horsemen, compared to 40,000 infantry and 3,000 horsemen on the Roman side.[6]

The Romans did indeed have the advantage in Hispania, but a defeat in that battle would mean the loss of all their previous gains. They were fortunate, and the battle ended with a great victory by Scipio. Any possibility of a Carthaginian counterattack was abandoned when their local allies, the powerful Turdetani in particular, deserted. Scipio pursued the fleeing enemy; Mago and Hasdrubal just managed to escape by sea with only 6,000 soldiers.

Following this battle, Cornelius Scipio sent his brother Lucius to Rome to announce that they had been victorious in the war and that Hispania was conquered. Some researchers claim that Scipio was too hasty in his declaration and that he might have even exaggerated.

The question is whether Scipio really meant to say that he had conquered all of Hispania. It is more likely that his intention had been to confirm that he had conquered the areas that were under Carthaginian control prior to the war. In addition, exaggerated and overstated descriptions concerning victories were common place in the Roman world (or any other society for that matter). It had been so before Scipio, and would continue after his time. The most prominent and relevant example is that of Julius Caesar's description of his victories when conquering Gaul. Once the war against the Carthaginians was over, Scipio launched attacks against several Iberian cities. The reasons for these attacks are specified in a speech by Scipio, quoted in the writings of Livius, were that these cities had helped in defeating Cnaeus and Publius Scipio during 211, and they had also assisted the Carthaginians in the war. The real reason was probably Scipio's intention to conquer any Hispanic region that had not been under Roman control, and turn it into a Roman province. Appianus mentions the establishment of the province of Italica, 9km northwest of present-day Seville, as evidence to these intended expansions. It seems that Scipio did not ask for consent of the Senate for founding the province, as he had done before when he set out on his own to conquer Carthago Nova. The great distance from Rome and his high position had allowed him to conduct himself in such a way.

Before returning triumphant to Rome, Scipio was forced to go to battle yet again, when his former allies, Indibilis and Mandonius, launched an attack against Rome's allies and the Roman forces. The revolt began when rumours had spread that Scipio had died from an illness. This was a large-scale revolt, and for a time, his allies had begun rethinking their next moves; his soldiers had begun to fear for their lives.

All the achievements in the war against the Carthaginians were at risk, but Scipio had swiftly defeated all the rebel chieftains in one battle and calm once again prevailed. Scipio had left as planned for Rome to participate in the election of the Consuls. There is no doubt that the vast amount of silver – 55,000kg – that Scipio Africanus brought with him as spoils from the Punic War and deposited in the State treasury, helped him in the elections.

Rome's attempts to expand its control in Hispania and the beginning of the Celtiberian War

This chapter discusses the first wars that Rome fought against the local tribes in Hispania; wars in which *praetors* and consuls commanded relatively small armies, which only rarely included more than 20,000 soldiers. The Romans had had to confront a tough enemy which used two fighting methods: 'conventional' and 'guerrilla'. This relates to the first years of the Roman wars in Hispania, the period in which the Roman presence becomes permanent and two provinces were established: Hispania Citerior and Hispania Ulterior.

By 205, the entire area of the former Carthaginian Hispania was under Roman control. An attempt by Indibilis to start another revolt was suppressed by the Roman garrisons with no need for reinforcement. There was no other force in Hispania which possessed the power to threaten Rome's interests, and although there was apparently no need for a military presence, the Roman army remained in the Iberian Peninsula.

Curchin believes that the fierce conflicts among the different tribes in the Iberian Peninsula had thwarted any attempt to sign treaties or establish kingdoms under the auspices of Rome. The Romans probably feared that the evacuation of their forces would provoke another Carthaginian invasion. During such an invasion, they could not rely on the local tribes, let alone the mobilization of Roman forces from the metropolis to Hispania, since it would require too much time. Therefore, the Romans did not see any way of holding on to Hispania, apart from maintaining a permanent presence and through direct control. This was manifested by the organization of the administration in this region, the founding of provinces and stationing a permanent garrison.

On the other hand, Richardson believes that other reasons had led to Rome's permanent presence in Hispania, in particular the Punic war, in which Rome had a distinct advantage in 206. Richardson thinks that the Romans feared a possible Gaelic invasion of Hispania, but he believes that this was improbable. The Roman conection with Hispania and its inhabitants, especially the Greeks, was stronger than one might think. These Iberian cities that were traditionally allies of Rome and the Greek cities in the peninsula had tipped the scales in favour of the Roman army's staying.

In 205, P. Scipio brought a delegation from Saguntum to the Senate in Rome, to express their gratitude, on behalf of the citizens, for the tremendous efforts that the Romans had invested in freeing them from the Carthaginians. The delegates also made offerings to Jupiter Optimus Maximus at his temple, and asked that the Senate approve the Roman presence in Hispania as well as benefits to the loyal people of Saguntum. Other cities, including Emporion, Terraco, Nova Carthago, and the colony of Italica, expressed the same wish.

However, Roman soldiers were among those who opposed the continuation of the Roman presence in Hispania. They protested against service in a remote area and claimed that following the triumph over the Carthaginians, there was no need to remain in Hispania. According to Livius, they were close to mutinying. According to Richardson, Scipio was the driving force behind Rome's decision to remain in Hispania, mainly due to economic reasons. Scipio decided that the rich gold and silver mines and the expanses of fertile land would remain under Roman control for the benefit of the State and also, possibly, for the benefit of his own family. Scipio and his family had gained much prestige because of Hispania, which was a potential source of high earnings in the near future.

When Scipio left Hispania in 206, the Senate was faced with a constitutional problem concerning that country. They had to decide how to deal with the reality in which the controlled area was so distant. There had been no precedents to such a situation in the history of the Roman Republic, and several attempts were made to find the correct law for the new situation. For several years, the status of the new territory was undecided, as was the authority of the Roman commanders-in-chief, sent to Hispania as governors. Sometimes, the authority of a pro-consular was debated, and at other times, the authority of a *pro-praetor*.

Either way, it can be said that during the elections for official position holders in 197, two additional *praetors*, M. Helvius and C. Sempronius Tuditanus, were elected to command two provinces in Hispania. The two provinces were: Hispania Citerior commanded by Tuditanus and Hispania Ulterior commanded by Helvius.

In keeping with Roman practice, there were no clear borders between the two provinces. There was no fixed marking but an estimated and flexible zone, which could be moved according to the operational requirements of the commanders. This border strip was situated in the area of Sierra Morena and south of Carthago Nova.

There could be several possible reasons for the division into two provinces. The first is that the Roman Senate was wary of placing too much power into the hands of one person, especially if that person was located far away from the centre of government. That meant, in effect, that one person would have autonomous control a large and rich province.

Another possible reason is the vast size of the area and the many challenges that such a commander would face: many of the indigenous tribes that lived there were considered by the Romans as unreliable.

In addition, there was also the option of a Carthaginian or Numidian invasion from the south, or by the Gaelic and Celtiberian tribes, such as the Sedetani, Ilergeti or Lusitanians, from the north and west.

Both of the two recently elected *praetors* arrived in their provinces with an army of 8,000 infantry soldiers and 400 horsemen. Soon after their arrival, these armies began fighting against the local tribes, as they had begun a series of widespread uprising throughout the two Hispanias. The causes of the uprising are unknown: Appianus makes the improbable suggestion that the Hispanic tribes had known that the Romans were busy fighting against Philip V of Macedon and the Gaelic tribes in the Po Valley.

In 197, Tuditanus of Hispania Citerior was killed in battle and the suppression of the uprising took a very heavy toll in Roman lives. When the Senate in Rome learned of these events it became very apprehensive. In 195, the Senate decided to send the consul M. Porcius Cato to Hispania, supported by an army of two Roman legions, 800 horsemen, reinforced with 15,000 Latin allies and twenty warships.

Cato's conduct in Hispania is known from the writings of Livius, who probably relied on the writings of Cato himself; therefore his words should not be taken at face value. Livius himself has written that Cato was not one to underestimate his own achievements, or one to not speak much of his own feats. Plutarchus was more blatant and said that Cato had never missed an opportunity to blow his own trumpet.

In modern research, there are differences of opinion concerning Cato's accomplishments. Astin doubts the veracity of writings by Cato and considers them as somewhat exaggerated. Richardson writes that descriptions originating from Cato that appear in works by Livius should be treated with caution, but he does not reject their credibility.

After a long waiting period, which was necessary to allow the recruitment of a force of some 25,000 soldiers and also to assemble a large fleet, Cato sailed from the port of Luna, south of Pisa. Also he had to wait for weather suitable for the long voyage. The fleet arrived at the port of the city of Emporion, in the north-eastern coast of Hispania, where the military force disembarked. Archaeological excavations in Empures have uncovered remains in the ancient layer, which are attributed to constructions associated with Cato's venture. It seems that Cato had built an army camp on the border of the Greek city. These remains also reveal that there had been a permanent Roman military presence in the city throughout the second century.

According to the works of Livius, Cato first decided not to use external suppliers, mostly Italian, and use local produce to provision the army in Hispania.[7] This was a revolutionary action, because Roman armies had always used their own provisions and suppliers to battlefront. The idea behind this was probably that if Cato succeeded, the army stationed in Hispania would be less dependent on support from Rome. In the future only military manpower was to be sent from Rome. One can say that this action by Cato marked the beginning of intensive exploitation of resources in the Iberian Peninsula by Rome. Over the years, his became a representation of the greed of Roman commanders-in-chief that were sent to Hispania.

Cato introduced additional changes in Hispania. He began using psychological-warfare tactics when negotiating with allies whose credibility seemed questionable. He employed the same method with his enemies. When representatives of the Ilergetes had arrived in Emporion, requesting his help, he ordered his men to board warships and prepare for war in order to help his ally. But once the Ilergete delegates had left, Cato ordered his men to disembark.

He achieved three objectives in one action: he secured the loyalty of the Ilergetes, intimidated the tribes that attacked the Ilergetes, and avoided going into battle and losing Roman soldiers.

Cato had introduced a regime of large-scale manoeuvres with a double objective: prepare his army for the future and frighten his enemies by spreading rumours about these manoeuvres. These together with pillaging campaigns had caused much friction with the local tribes. Livius writes that the tribes around Emporion – where Cato's training base was located – which had a long tradition of loyalty to Rome, had rebelled because of the numerous manoeuvres and looting by his army.[8]

Cato had employed psychological warfare numerous times while serving in Hispania, for example, when initiating an attack against the Indigetes. When the Indigetes had almost succeeded in breaking the Roman lines, Cato sent small units behind enemy lines thus frightening them and causing a hasty retreat. Eventually, Cato won the battle and used a reserve legion that he prepared in advance, to conquer the fortified settlements of the Indigetes and slaughter the inhabitants.

Cato had used this victory to continue his progress westward, towards Terraco. There he had to face the possibility of being delayed for a long period, due to a large number of fortified villages and cities where, if he attacked, his army could possibly suffer heavy losses. But Cato succeeded in obtaining the surrender of his enemies by using a ploy: he sent representatives to each individual town who threatened that it would anihilated unless the populace destroyed the walls and surrendered. This ploy succeeded and all the settlements in the area surrendered and suffered no Roman losses.

It is obvious that Cato had operated throughout Hispania, without any regard to the borders between the two provinces. After he had won the above victories, he headed south to help the *praetor* P. Manlius, who at that time was fighting the Turdetani tribe in the south of Hispania. The Turdetani had been defeated in the wars against P. Manlius, until they recruited 10,000 Celtiberian mercenaries which they deployed to gain the advantage. The grave situation for P. Manlius in the south required Cato to gather together all of his soldiers before setting out to help him.

Cato's forces also included the soldiers stationed in the newly-conquered territories. This was a very perilous move on his part, because it exposed his home front to attacks and rebellions in areas where his control had not yet been fully secured. Cato succeeded in warding off the Celtiberians, and immediately began making use of his skills for out-manoeuvring his enemies and using the art of diplomacy. He offered the Celtiberians to choose one of three options: receive double the money offered by the Turdetani and change to his side; leave the battlefield and return safely home, or meet him in battle and pay for this choice with their lives. While the Celtiberian leaders were holding debates on the best course of action, Cato launched an attack into the heart of Celtiberian territory in an attempt to cut off the mercenaries from their home base and sources of supply. Cato also fought against the Lacetani tribe in the Ebro Valley and conquered the Celtiberian city of Saguntia. He would take prisoners from those that he had fought as an 'insurance policy' even before the delivery of his demand for the walls to be demolished. After acheiving his objectives in the autumn, Cato returned to his winter camp in Emporion.

Cato is considered as the first to introduce regulations for the collection of taxes in Hispania in order to finance the Roman army. He was mainly involved in exploiting the iron and silver mines of Hispania Citerior. Cato had, in fact, prompted the process of exploitating the economic resources of Hispania by the Romans.

When he returned to Rome, the Senate has expressed its gratitude to Cato by holding a *triumpho* (victory parade), and a three day celebration as a gesture of *supplicatio* (gratitude) to the gods.

The Senate, which probably relied only on Cato's account of the events, disbanded his army of two veteran and experienced legions, and auxiliary forces. The next governors of Hispania would suffer gravely from the consequences of this move.

In 195, following Cato's return to Rome, rebellions occured throughout Hispania, which Scipio Nasica, the son of C. Scipio, who was nominated as the governor of Hispania Ulterior, suppressed. More rebellions occured and the governors of Hispania Ulterior and Hispania Citerior took part in the attempts to suppress them. Sextus Digitus, the governor of Hispania Citerior, was defeated in the region between the river Ebro and the Pyrenees which, according to Cato, was thought to be under the control of the Romans.

From the correspondence between C. Flaminius, who replaced Digitus in Hispania Citerior and the Senate, it is evident how unstable the situation in Hispania had become, and how little information the Senate had received about the events in Hispania. Flaminius sent a request for additional forces due to the difficult situation in the field, but the Senate claimed, from information based on reports from Cato, that the province was supposed to be in control and therefore the forces he had were quite sufficient.

Flaminus together with M. Fluvius Nobilior, governor of Hispania Ulterior, fought against numerous tribes throughout Hispania. In 192, they defeated a coalition of tribes the Vaccei, Vectones and Celtiberians in a battle near Toletum (present-day Toledo), and this is the first reference to it in sources.[9]

The border between the two provinces was well-defined in the coastal area, but inland it was unclear, and each governor who had battled against the tribes, did so based on his needs and the conditions in the field. In 190, for example, L. Aemilius Paulus fought against the Lusitanians in the north and west of Hispania Ulterior. He defeated them and acquired a vast stock of booty, which included a large amount of gold. He brought temporary peace to Hispania. In 189, he issued a decree – preserved on an inscription discovered in archaeological excavations – that freed the slaves of Hasta Regia, who lived in a tower, an act which was probably considered shameful in the eyes of the Romans. It is possible that these people were locals who were not really slaves but were dependent on their masters, which explains the fact that they were also land owners. The decree also specified that they were allowed to keep their land and property, for as long 'as the Senate and people in Rome should please'. This last sentence proves that there were, after all, limits to the authority bestowed on the governors in Hispania, and that the Senate held the overall authority to approve or annul agreements between the governor and the different local tribes.

The 80s of the second century were full of military campaigns in the two Hispanic provinces. The Romans were defeated and two governors, whose names are not mentioned in the sources, were killed in battle. But in general there was Roman progress in all fronts. Victories were achieved in the Upper Ebro Valley during 186 and the Toledo area in 185. Q. Flaccus, the governor of Hispania Citerior, achieved a great victory in a battle against the Lusones in 181 while waiting for his replacement, T. Sempronius Gracchus. The Lusones had revolted, but since they were unable to defeat Flaccus on the battlefield, they entrenched themselves around the city of Complega and tried to negotiate with him. Flaccus refused, and they had to retreat and settle for ransacking other tribes in the region.

Following his suppression of the revolt, Q. Flaccus set out on another military campaign against the Celtiberians. He had achieved nothing other than enrage the Celtiberian tribes because of his plundering, due to a lack of real victory in battle. Flaccus sent his legate, L. Minucius, to Rome to inform the Senate of his impressive success in Hispania and also to request its approval for him to return to Rome and bring back his entire army. S. Gracchus protested and claimed it would be an irresponsible act to release the veterans. If it had been approved, Gracchus would have had to confront the Celtiberians with only two legions of new recruits. The Celtiberians enjoyed the reputation of being belligerent and rebellious, and Gracchus feared his own future in Hispania. After deliberations, the Senate decided to release only the soldiers who had served in Hispania since 187, as well as those who excelled in battles against the Celtiberians. Following that decision, Gracchus only needed to recruit one legion of new recruits, some half of the forces required to fill his duty in Hispania.

Documentation regarding the military campaigns of S. Gracchus, governor of Hispania Citerior, and Postumius Albinus, governor of

Hispania Ulterior, is inadequate. The documentation from the year 179 is haphazard and unclear; that concerning the year 178 is lost, and there is only an epitaph by Livius. Albinus and S. Gracchus agreed that he would fight the Celtiberians and Albinus the Lusitanians and Vaccei. The exact geographic route of these campaigns is unknown. The only piece of information available is that in 178, S. Gracchus had established a colony in the Upper Ebro Valley. As agreed between the two governors, S. Gracchus defeated the Celtiberians and Albinus defeated the Lusitanians, and probably the Vaccei.[10]

In written sources (Polybius, Livius and Appianus), S. Gracchus is also mentioned because of the agreements he had signed with the ambassadors of the different Hispanic tribes. These agreements were based on mutual respect between the two sides, and similar to those signed by Scipio Africanus decades earlier. Appianus wrote that these tribes had become 'friends of Rome' by virtue of the agreements that S. Gracchus had signed with them. Another tradition that is related to the outcome of the agreements states that the minute S. Gracchus left Hispania revolts broke out, yet it is actually doubtful, since according to the sources the agreements were signed based on the will of the two parties, and Hispania had gained many years of relative peace.

S. Gracchus was a pioneer of establishing administrative procedures in Hispania. According to the agreements, each tribe was obligated to provide auxiliary soldiers to the Roman army and pay taxes. It can be said that these agreements were used by his son T. Gracchus, as a guarantee for the family's integrity. In 137 they probably even saved his life, when the Numantines were at the brink of destroying the Roman army.

S. Gracchus was also introduced the 'five per cent' tax, at the end of the 60s of the second century. The tax was levied on farmers and charged them at 5 per cent of their annual wheat crop to be delivered to the local Roman government. This tax was introduced in order to ensure the supply of food to the army without the need to receive supplies from Rome or sign agreements with Italian or other contractors.

S. Gracchus has basically applied and institutionalized Cato's intentions in this matter. In addition, Gracchus allowed the Celtiberians to fortify their settlements, but not to build new ones.

Prior to Gracchus' triumphant return to Rome, he founded a city and named it after him, Gracchuris. In doing so, he set a precedent for the future throughout the Roman Empire at the time of the Republic, and in the *Principate* period in particular.

S. Gracchus had succeeded in bringing a rare and relative peace, for a certain period of time, to Hispania by using military victories at first followed by an intelligent use of diplomacy. Peace lasted until the mid-50s of the second century. The prevailing peace led to the reduction of the Roman army in Hispania to half its size, and then included only one legion in each province (instead of two previously).

In the 70s of the second century, the Senate's attention was drawn almost entirely to the wars in the east. Firstly, Hispania was relatively quiet, and secondly, a war broke out against Perseus, king of Macedonia. Most of the Republic's resources – economic and human (soldiers and especially officers) – were sent to the war. In 172, due to internal politics, the *praetors* who were sent to Hispania were denied the right to go to the more important war in the east.[11] In 171, only one *praetor* was sent to Hispania to govern both the provinces. Only in 167, when the war against Perseus had ended successfully, did the Senate revert, according to the Roman point of view, to the pre-war format and sent again two *praetors* to Hispania.

It can be said that Roman history in Hispania was riddled with wars, from the time of Scipio Africanus' return to Rome in 196 until S. Gracchus' return to Rome in 178. During these years, twenty-three *praetors*, one ex-*praetor* and one consul had served in Hispania.

The vast majority of these were involved in wars against the different tribes, apart from the following: Ap. Claudius Pulcher, who in 195 was untimeously replaced by Cato; L.Plautius Hipseus and P. Iunius Brutus, who were replaced in 189 because they refused to start a war; and P. Sempronius Longus, who ruled in the years 184-183 and was ill for most of his tenure.

Triumph in the war had awarded the commander-in-chief with much prestige and wealth, since the achievements were considered more personal than those of the State (the Senate); but when these commanders returned to Rome, it was the Senate that determined whether to hold a victory procession in their honour. The criterion for a procession seems to be aggressiveness on the battlefield, whether justified or not, which brought more prestige and respect to the victor. This was held in higher regard by the Senate than newly-conquered territories or peacemaking between Rome and its enemies.

Scipio Aemilianus in Hispania: The Numantine and Lusitanian Wars

This chapter discusses the most difficult period for the Romans throughout their wars in Hispania. The new reality in which Roman armies fought abroad, and were sometimes engaged in several military campaigns simultaneously, was an important factor in the events that led to the wars that will be discussed here, especially the Lusitanian War. The government's difficulty dealing with this reality was the main reason for the controversial behaviour of Roman commanders in the field; the most prominent cases were those of S. Galba and L. Lucullus. This shows the importance of a central figure, a great leader such as Scipio Aemilianus, who could lead to victory, in spite of initial bad conditions. As for the Numantine war, this is the only time in the Roman wars in Hispania when the central arena was the siege of a city. This was a long siege, during which all the components of warfare were brought into play, including a serious use of war machines.

The revolts that occured throughout Hispania between the 50s and 30s of the second century, sparked large-scale wars, some of the most brutal in which the Roman army was involved. These wars were the last attempt by the Celtiberians and Lusitanians to get rid of the Roman conqueror, and there were times when it seemed that this objective was within reach.

The customary method of appointing governors in Hispania had also undergone a change. Since 197, it had become customary to appoint *praetors* as governors of the two provinces, but from then on most governors were to be consuls or ex-consuls. Due to the deterioration of the situation in both Hispanic provinces, the Roman Senate decided to send a consular army of two legions to each province, instead of a *praetor* with one legion. This had led to a change in the date of the consular appointment, so that they would have sufficient time to complete their mission in Hispania. The consuls were appointed in January, instead of March, as had been customary. It can be concluded that the reasons for this constitutional change were the countless difficulties that the consuls encountered when attempting to recruit forces for the war in Hispania, as well as the difficulties when confronting the different tribes in the Iberian Peninsula.

The primary source for information regarding these wars is Appianus. Although it is difficult to know what his sources were, his descriptions seem to be coherent and consistent, and there is no reason to question their reliability. He described the wars geographically: first the Celtiberian revolt in Hispania Ulterior and then the Numantine War in Hispania Citerior and each is described in chronological order.

Livius provided only two epitaphs, one from a manuscript and the other from a papyrus from Oxyrhyncus.

The wars began in the year 155-154, when the Lusitanians and Vettones revolted in Hispania Ulterior. Some 6,000 Roman soldiers were killed in this revolt, including the *quaestor* of the province. *Praetor* L. Mummius, governor of the province, overpowered the rebels, after he had been defeated suffering the loss of 9,000 of his soldiers in August, 153. The revolt in Hispania Citerior began in 154, as a result of a deterioration in relations between Rome and the Celtiberian city of Segeda. According to Appianus, Segeda was a large and important city, which belonged to the Belli tribe and it was among those cities that had signed an agreement with T. Gracchus in 179. It seems that Segeda headed a federation of Celtiberian city-states which had refused to pay taxes to the Roman governor and also provide auxiliary soldiers for his army. Archaeological excavations in Planos de Mara, on the banks of the river Perehiles, a tributary of the river Jalon, have uncovered remains which seem to give a definite identification of the city. In the ancient layers, called by the diggers Segeda-1, the remains of a city destroyed in 153 and rebuilt (Segeda-2), as an Iberian-Roman city, have been discovered.

The Roman Senate appointed the consul Q. Fluvius Nobilior as the governor of Hispania Citerior, with orders to crush the Celtiberian revolt. The appointment took effect on 1 January, instead of 1 March, as had been customary. This can be explained in two ways; the least convincing of the two is the severity of the situation in the province. It is hard to assume that the Senate had anticipated what would happen, as it probably considered the Celtiberian revolt just as another one in a long line of Hispanic uprisings. The other, which is more likely, is that at that time there was a shortage of provinces with an *imperium* potential. The wars against the Macedonians and Seleucids had ended and with them, for the time being, the possibilities of gaining military glory in the east.

P. Nobilior was sent to Hispania Citerior at the head of an army of 30,000 soldiers. The people of Segeda, who did not have a chance to fortify their city, escaped and sought refuge with the Arevaci. This tribe had defeated the Romans in a battle on 23 August, and then consolidated positions in Numantia. The forces of P. Nobilior recovered quickly, and following a pursuit built a camp twenty-four *stadias* (4.3km) from the city. Nobilior besieged Numantia, but this failed. (Some 30km south of Numantia in Fuerte Almaza, the site of a large Roman army camp has been discovered, and attributed, based on numismatics, to the Nobilior campaign against Numantia.) The defeat of his army at a battle in the area of Xuama and the slaughter of a unit sent to recruit allies from the neighbouring tribes, convinced P. Nobilior to retreat to his winter camp. C. Claudius Marcellus, who was P. Nobilior's replacement, tried to handle the revolt in a different way. His soldiers raided the agricultural lands of the Arevaci and their allies, until they begged him to stop the fighting and revert to the previous agreements that had been signed with Gracchus.

However, the Roman Senate thwarted the move; it demanded a *deditio* (total surrender) and not peace treaties. Once the attempt to reach an agreement had failed, the battles were resumed, until C. Marcellus besieged the city of Negobriga. At the beginning of 151 the city surrendered, the war against the Arevaci and their Titthi and Belli allies was over, before Lucullus, the replacement for Marcellus, arrived in Hispania Citerior.

The feeling of discontent in the Senate concerning the attempt by Marcellus to resolve the problem of the many revolts in Hispania by diplomatic means, was also manifested in the appointment of new governors. These were L. Licinius Lucullus and Servius Sulpicius Galba, as governors of Hispania Citerior and Hispania Ulterior, respectively, both were members of the 'hawks' faction in Rome.

The arrival of Lucullus to the province marks the beginning of one of the darkest chapters in the Roman conquest of Hispania. Lucullus came to govern – like his predecessors and those that followed – in order to gain military glory that would enable him to accumulate wealth and gain political power on his return to Rome. Unfortunately, he discovered it to be calm in the province; the Arevaci had already surrendered to Marcellus, and the other tribes were observing the peace. If we rely on descriptions by Appianus, the avaricious Lucullus had begun his tenure by declaring war on the Vaccei, which had signed a peace treaty with Rome.

Lucullus won a battle near the city of Cauca, and the people accepted the surrender terms that he dictated: they paid 100 silver talents, and surrendered hostages and horsemen to him. Once the people of Cauca had fulfilled his demands, he slaughtered all the men and plundered the city. Since then, the people of the area no longer believed the word of Lucullus, and he had to fight every time that he wanted to obtain any required monies. His killing and plundering campaign ended in Palencia when his attempt to conquer the city failed, and he returned to his winter camp in Turdetania. Excavations at a site near Tariego de Cerrato of the most ancient layer of destruction have identified this as being from the war.

In the spring, Lucullus joined forces with Galba in the war against the Lusitanians. The two armies attacked the Lusitanians using a successful pincer movement, which forced them to seek terms for surrender. The Lusitanians had turned to Galba, and he promised them more fertile lands in return for their land. Galba ordered them to divide into three groups, and then camp at a distance from each other. He then ordered his soldiers to attack the Lusitanians, group after group: thousands were slaughtered and any survivors were sold into slavery in Gaul. Rome condemned the actions ordered by Galba, which were deemed inappropriate for a Roman noble, but Appianus implies that he managed to evade punishment by paying a bribe.

The Romans very quickly felt the consequences of Galba's actions. Viriathus, a leader and son of the Lusitanian nobility who survived the massacre, led a 'national' uprising against the Romans in Hispania. According to Paterculus, the military campaign that the Romans had led in order to crush the uprising was very harsh and shameful. The Romans suffered more failures than successes in this war, and the final victory of the conquerors was achieved not through courage in battle, but due to another act of treachery and murder.

The uprising led by Viriathus began in the year 147and achieved a first important victory in a battle near Tribola in which C. Vetilius, the Roman governor, was killed. This success excited the rebels, and the fire of revolt spread throughout Hispania Ulterior. In the year 144, the consul Q. Fabius Maximus Aemilianus ended the raids by Viriathus after winning the battle of Urso. Viriathus turned to the Celtiberians – who had signed a peace treaty with Marcellus seven years earlier – and requested them to join the war against the Romans, but the Romans acted quickly and thwarted his initiative. The government in Rome identified the turbulence in Hispania and acted accordingly; the famous orator and philosopher C. Laelius Sapiens, governor of Hispania Citerior, was replaced by a respected military figure, the consul Q. Caecilius Metellus, one of the conquerors of Macedonia. Metellus had successfully attacked the Arevaci rebels while they were busy with the harvest, but like Sapiens he did not succeed in conquering the city of Numantia, which had become the symbol of rebellion against Rome and therefore, an important site.

The Romans became more and more entangled in the war against the Celtiberian tribes led by Numantia. In 139, the pro-consul Q. Pompeius was forced to sign an agreement – after being repeatedly attacked by the Numantines – the terms of which were not that convenient to Rome. Two years later, the consul G. Hostilius Mancinus was ambushed by Celtiberian warriors and was forced to surrender in order to save the lives of his people.

The Senate in Rome refused to sign the two agreements signed in Hispania, claiming that they were disgraceful, and even sent Mancinus, naked and in heavy chains, as a 'present' to the Celtiberians.

At that time, Rome had won victories and suffered defeats in the war against Viriathus in Hispania Ulterior. The consul Q. Fabius Maximus Servilianus arrived in Hispania with a force of African horsemen and elephants. In a battle that took place near the village of Ittuca, Servilianus defeated Viriathus; but a hasty pursuit of the fleeing Lusitanians turned into a counterattack that pushed the Romans back to the walls of the village.

Viriathus had suffered many losses in these battles, but he soon recovered and defeated Servilianus again; this time it was a crushing victory near to the village of Erisana which was under siege by the Romans. Servilianus was forced to sign a peace treaty, which was surprisingly ratified by the Senate in Rome. It seemed that Rome had finally become tired of war, and the legislators were relieved to sign a treaty which declared the end of hostilities, and also that Viriathus became a friend Rome.

Servilianus was replaced by his brother, Q. Servilius Caepio, who convinced the Senate to annul the treaty, which he deemed shameful, with Viriathus and renew the war against him. Caepio had defeated the Lusitanians in Carpentia and forced them to retreat. In the year 139, Caepio attacked the Vettones and Gallaeci, the forefathers of the Gallegos, neighbours and allies of the Lusitanians from the north and east, who now appear for the first time in historic sources. M. Popillius Laenas, governor of Hispania Citerior, also participated in the battles.

Viriathus found himself surrounded by two consular armies and tried to negotiate with the Romans. At first he tried with Popillius, but when he demanded that Viriathus surrender, he made a subsequent attempt with Caepio, but was murdered.

Researchers accept the version by Appianus, according to which Caepio bribed the Lusitanian representatives to murder Viriathus. However, it should be mentioned that Diodorus Siculus had written a different version, and the names of the Lusitanian representatives are different from those mentioned by Appianus; more importantly he claims that it was the Lusitanians that offered to murder Viriathus to win the favour of the Romans.

Iunius Brutus, who was Caepio's replacement in Hispania Ulterior, carried out several raids against the Lusitanians. Firstly, Brutus had to overcome the reluctance of his soldiers who feared crossing the Lethe (there were those who saw the river as the gateway to the world of the dead). This he did by crossing the river himself carrying the banner at the head of the army. He then won the battle against the Galaic army.

According to Strabo, Brutus fortified the city of Olisipo (present-day Lisbon). Apparently, Brutus used the city as his base for the war against the Lusitanians and Galaics in the northwest of the Iberian Peninsula.

While the Roman army fought in north-east Hispania against the

Lusitanians and their allies, another military campaign in Hispania Citerior against the city of Numantia, managed to keep the flame of the Celtiberian revolt alive. The war was hard for the Romans forcing them to take impulsive action, such as the attack on the Vaccei by M. Emilius Lepidus, which only made matters worse.

Lepidus had tried to conquer Palantia, claiming that its people were helping Numantia. The siege of Palantia failed and the Senate ordered Lepudus to return in disgrace, since he had involved Rome in an unnecessary war. His replacement, Q. Calpurnius Piso, also tried to conquer Palantia and failed. Piso was probably too frightened to attack the more powerful Numantia, and instead tried Palantia.

The war against Numantia was not progressing in favour of the Romans. According to Livius, the Numantine War was characterized by failures of unskilled Roman commanders-in-chief that brought shame on the Roman people.

It was hard to recruit soldiers and it was even harder to recruit commanders, because Romans were frightened of going to Hispania. Reports of the fierce fighting in the peninsula deterred them, this had never happened before.

The Senate in Rome had become weary of the many failures of the Roman army in Hispania. In the year 134, Publius Scipio Africanus Aemilianus, the destroyer of Carthage, was appointed a consul for a second time, and his appointment involved legislation to remove the age limit for consuls. The Senate appointed Aemilianus as the commander-in-chief of all Roman forces in Hispania for one purpose: to defeat Numantia.

Many researchers have dealt with the question of identifying the battlefields in the area of Numantia, especially identifying the Roman siege works around the city. At the beginning of the twentieth century, Schulten identified some of the siege works and also he identified a Roman army camp at Renieblas, 8km south of Numantia, as the winter camp of Nobilior. New research following the excavations does confirm that the second layer of the camp dates to the years 153-152. The most ancient layer is dated to the beginning of the second century, probably the P. Cato period. It should be mentioned that at present, most of the Roman siege works opposite Numantia have been uncovered, although

opinions differ as to the dating of the different elements. Among the
fortifications so far uncovered is the *circumvallum* (perimeter wall),
two large camps that housed one legion each,[12] and seven smaller army
camps, also two fortresses.

The army of Scipio included two legions, and also Italian and
Iberian auxiliary forces that had been recruited from the tribes aligned
to Rome. He also received significant assistance from Iugurtha and his
Numidian horsemen.

He was accompanied by Polybius, whose works – especially those
quoted by Appianus – serve as our main source of information in
regard to these wars.

Scipio had arrived in Hispania and began his tenure by 'cleansing' the
army. He drove out the traders and prostitutes that followed the camp,
and cancelled several 'luxuries' including sleeping in beds. Scipio then
held a series of intensive training programmes, which included trench
digging and building fortifications. Scipio also dealt with the most serious
problem in the army: the poor level of discipline now endemic in Roman
soldiers stationed in Hispania who suffered from fatigue following years
of failure and constant battle.

In spite of enemy provocations Scipio was not tempted to go into
battle, he would do do only when he felt that his army was ready. He also
managed to survive several ambushes laid by the Numantines. When
Scipio came to the conclusion that his army was ready, he launched
attacks against the Arevaci and Vaccei. After the battle he confiscated
their grain to feed his army, and destroyed the rest. Scipio then set out to
Numantia, together with forces sent by Iugurtha, king of Numidia, where
he cut the lines of supply before setting siege to the city.[13] He ordered a
trench to be dug around the city and two parallel walls, with a perimeter
of forty-eight *stadia*, to be built. The outer wall was constructed to defend
the soldiers from outside attempts to free or reinforce the besieged city.
Between the two walls there were seven camps; a number of look-out
towers were integrated into the walls.

The Numantines had tried several times to provoke a battle but
Scipio, with 60,000 soldiers, avoided any reaction and waited for the
right moment. Also, he refused several attempts by the defenders of

the city to reach an agreement to lift the siege, and was focused on an unconditional surrender. The citizens of Numantia were resolute in their revolt despite the harsh conditions; they barely survived.

The city surrendered after eight months of siege due to hunger, and also due the fact that all attempts to reach an agreement with Scipio failed. The city was burned to the ground. Many of its citizens were sold as slaves, but some had chosen to take their own lives in order to retain their freedom. A number were sent to Rome to take part in a victory procession for Scipio. Although a few voices in the Senate protested against the burning of Numantia, the general atmosphere in Rome was of relief and satisfaction.

The fall and destruction of Numantia was a severe blow to the Celtiberian people. Their opposition to Rome had continued – intermittently and in varying intensity – for many years, until the arrival of Augustus; but the fall of Numantia had become a symbol of the beginning of the surrender of Roman control over the Iberian Peninsula.

Between the Celtiberian and Cantabrian Wars, the Revolt of Sertorius

The events referred to in the title had taken place following several years of relative peace and intermittent military activity, which ended with the Roman civil wars; Hispania being the main theatre. This book will not deal with the battles amongst the Roman armies themselves, apart from the episode of a revolt organized by Sertorius. This was characterized by a massive recruitment of local forces, which had formed the main component of the rebelling faction in the army for a very long time. Sertorius, the revolt leader, had used a variety of fighting methods, including guerrilla, against the army.

The period in question – fifty years – between the conquest of Numantia by Scipio Aemilianus and the revolt by Sertorius was barely discussed in historic sources. Appianus, who had described in great length the Lusitanian and Numantine Wars, barely wrote anything about this period. Richardson believes that the descriptions of these wars had been the climax of writings by Appianus, and therefore he preferred to use only the minimum detail about what had followed. However, we cannot deny the possibility that Appianus simply did not have enough information to write at length about this period.

Following the Celtiberians and Lusitanians Wars, vast territories were added to the area under the control of Rome.[14] In order to restore order to these regions, the Senate sent ten governors to Hispania to serve as a control committee. It is hard to know the nature of their work, since there is no documented evidence, and there is no further mention of them in the sources. In addition, there are no changes to the administrative structure in Hispania, which could be attributed to their actions. Appianus is, in effect, the only source that mentions them.

There is little evidence about the events in Hispania in the last two decades of the second century. It is known that the consul Quintus Caecilius Metellus, governor of Hispania Citerior, had fought against pirates who attacked ships and the coastal settlements of the peninsula, in the year 123. These pirates probably originated from Sardinia and south Gaul, and had set up bases in the Balearic Islands, from where they set out on their raids.

Florus described them as barbarians and said that they used to attack merchant ships using small primitive vessels.

The consul Metellus defeated the pirates with relative ease. Once the war against them was over, Metellus seized the opportunity and conquered the Balearic Islands. He moved 3,000 Roman citizens, who lived in Hispania Citerior, to the islands and founded two colonies Palma and Pollentia on Majorca. In the year 121, in appreciation of his triumph over the pirates, he was honoured with a victory procession in Rome and awarded the title 'Balearicus'.

In the year 114, Gaius Marius was appointed as the governor of Hispania Ulterior. He treated groups of outlaws, who threatened the welfare and property of Hispanic citizens, with an iron fist. Until the end of the second century, several revolts had taken place in that area, usually initiated by the Lusitanians. In the year 101, M. Marius, the brother of the consul G. Marius, together with his allies the Celtiberians delivered a crushing defeat on the Lusitanians from which they never recovered.

Revolts throughout the two Hispanic provinces had taken place on a relatively small scale in the 90s of the first century. The Celtiberians and

Lusitanians revolted again, but unlike the wars of the mid-second century, it was obvious that the Roman government in Hispania was very stable and not on the verge of collapse.

The government in Rome probably did not consider these revolts as a great danger. The evidence is that the Roman Senate did not even bother to send consuls to Hispania. However, we must not forget the fact that at that time, the Cimbri and Teutoni threatened the north of the Appenine Peninsula, and the Iugurtha War was in its final stages. The order of priorities for the Senate in Rome was therefore, very clear and reasonable.

In spite of the this, the most serious threat to the stability of the government in the Republic arose at the end of the 80s in that century. This time, the threat was formed internally from among the ranks of the Roman army, and it arrived from Hispania.

Quintus Sertorius was a veteran of the Cambrian wars. He served under G. Marius in northern Italy and was a military tribune to consul Titus Didius when he was in Hispania at the beginning of the first century. He had also played an important role in the slave wars that took place later in Roman-controlled regions of Italy.

Sertorius supported the Marius side in his struggle against Lucius Cornelius Sulla. Marius then appointed Sertorius as the governor of Hispania Citerior, as a pro-consul. But when Sulla rose to power in Rome, Marius was banished into exile and Sertorius was forced to escape and settle in North Africa. Florus considered the revolt by Sertorius as a direct continuation of the confrontation between Marius and Sulla.

Sertorius was in Africa when the Lusitanians suggested that he assume the role of commander-in-chief to lead them in a revolt against the Romans. Sertorius, who saw this as a chance to fight against Sulla, accepted. He had moved to Hispania, and began to recruit officers from the Marius side, to build an army that was based on a group of Roman officers and soldiers who led the Iberians. He also accepted deserters from the Roman army, citizens of Roman colonies in Hispania and refugees from the Populares faction. Sertorius had set a precedent in Roman military history. This was the first time that a Roman commander-in-chief had set up an army the majority of which were 'barbarian' warriors. It seems that a successful combination of leadership and chicanery turned Sertorius into a respected figure, with an aura that bordered mystical reverence. The forces of Sertorius had helped him stand firm against the two consular armies sent by Sulla. For eight years, he succeeded in embarrassing Sulla and endangered his regime.

Sulla sent Q. Caecilius Metellus Pius, the second consul of the year 79, to crush the revolt. Archaeologists attribute the building of the expansive camp at Caceres El Viejo to Metellus, and it is customary to identify this site with Castra Caecilia, which is mentioned by Pliny the Elder. This rectangular-shaped camp is approximately 650m long and 370m wide; a camp large enough for one self-contained legion. Archaeologists have identified the *praetorium* (command building), the *quaestorium* (logistics building), the *horreum* (supplies warehouses), the barracks and several artisan workshops including a bakery, kitchen, a shoemaker's workshop and a blacksmith's. Metellus was a conservative old aristocrat who did not like 'new people'. His military education was focused on conventional warfare; an army fighting against another army, a legion against a falange. Sertorius, who had already fought in Hispania, had excellent knowledge of the terrain. Sertorius made his battle plan based on the lessons learned from previous wars in Hispania: in reality Metellus had no chance. Metellus had no experience of guerrilla warfare tactics and would not risk a direct confrontation with Sertorius. He began fighting, as did his father in the year 109, by using the 'scorched earth' tactic. But, unfortunately for Metellus, this tactic did not work according to his plans. Local people who witnessed their land and crops being destroyed by this tactic did not support Metellus, and neither did he manage to defeat Sertorius in battle. Sertorius was much faster than Metellus, and efficiently used intelligence to counter every move made by Metellus.

Sertorius was at the height of his power in the year 78. Most of the Hispanic peoples were loyal to him, and all the soldiers – fifty-three cohorts of Italians who once identified politically with Marius, (these had managed to escape from the forces of Sulla, after the failed revolt by the consul M. Aemilius Lepidus in the north of the peninsula) now marched under the flag of Sertorius.

At that time, the central government was probably located in the Navarra area of northern Hispania. Two inscriptions dated to the years 76 and 74, which relate to the rule of Sertorius, were discovered in this area. The first inscription found was at the camp in Aranguren and the second at a site adjacent to Pamplona (Roman *Pompelo*). Sertorius is referred to as a pro-consul in these inscriptions.

The fact that Sertorius had gathered large forces prompted grave concern in the Senate due to the possibility of an invasion of Rome. Therefore, the senators decided to send Cnaeus Pompeius to Hispania. He was in his twenties at that time, with no military achievements of any importance.

Pompeius arrived in Hispania during the autumn of the year 77. At first Sertorius did not react; he was busy with building a 'shadow senate' as a counter to the Senate in Rome. But when some of the tribes, who had feared the new Roman army, defected to Pompeius and Metellus, Sertoius prepared for war against the Roman commanders. At the beginning, the two sides had both defeats and victories. In one battle, Sertorius dealt a severe defeat to Pompeius, who lost 10,000 of his soldiers and their equipment in one day. At a battle in the area of Italica, Metellus defeated Hirtuleius, deputy to Sertorius. In the spring of 75, there was another battle in the Valencia area, but the outcome was not conclusive. Pompeius set out on a reckless attack, and was on the verge of defeat, but Metellus managed, at the last moment and with great difficulty, to save the day. Both sides retreated after suffering heavy losses – some 10,000 soldiers from each side. Metellus again saved Pompeius from defeat a second time in a battle that took place in Sagunto.

As the fighting continued, it became harder for Sertorius to keep up with the reinforcement rate of the two armies from Rome. However, Metellus and Pompeius did receive supplies on a regular basis, as the stream of desertions from Sertorius' army had grown stronger. Sertorius turned to guerrilla warfare tactics, but the tribesmen lacked the patience and persistence required for this type of fighting. The outcome was that the number of Celtiberian deserters had grown significantly, and his relationship with the Italian officers and soldiers under his command had deteriorated. Sertorius, after his Celtiberian allies deserted, retreated to north-east Hispania wounded in body and pride. There in the year 72, he attended a banquet given by his deputy Marcus Perpenna and was murdered by his Italian officers who had been incited by Perpenna. According to Appianus and Florus, Perpenna appointed himself as the leader of the army. It would take another year for Pompeius to finally defeat Perpenna and the soldiers who had remained true to Sertorius, even after his death. Pompeius returned victorious to Rome in the year 71, and coins were minted to commemorate his triumphs in Hispania, although he had never defeated Sertorius in battle, and had been saved many times by Metellus.

A short period of relative peace prevailed in Hispania following the end of the war against Sertorius. This peace came to an end in the year 61, when Gaius Iulius Caesar was appointed the governor of Hispania Ulterior.

Caesar was interested in glory that would guarantee his further political progress, and he also needed money to pay off his debts. He had recruited another legion and launched a military campaign in the Iberian Peninsula. He instigated a rapid military attack against the Lusitanians and Callaeci and conquered the entire Atlantic coast, from the south to the city of Brigantium (La Coruña, Galicia). Caesar conquered and plundered many settlements, but did not leave a permanent garrison in place. It is possible that the Lomba Do Canho fortress in central Portugal was one of the settlements. The site, which had been in use for a short period of time, is dated to the second third of the first century. Archaeologists have uncovered the headquarters, bath house, large storehouses, cooking stoves, and furnaces in the artisanal workshops, and barracks. Many small items have been found which indicate that it was a Roman military camp. Another site attributed to the same military campaign is Alcáçova de Santarém, located on high ground above the river Tagus. Archaeologists agree that the first layer of settlement is identified with Scallabis, which Pliny the Elder mentions as the city Caesar built and named Scalabis Praesidium Iulium after himself. It seems that a period of relative peace prevailed again, following Caesar's campaign. In the three decades that followed, between the years 56-26, Hispania served as the theatre for some very difficult wars. Since these wars focused on the interests of Roman citizens, the local population were of secondary importance; therefore, they had a minor impact on the continuation of the Roman conquest of Hispania and the establishment of the Roman control in the peninsula.

The Cantabrian and Asturian Wars

This chapter covers the final phase in the long campaign by Rome to conquer the Iberian Peninsula, and illustrates how all the resources of the empire were placed at the disposal of the leader, as part of a new political order. As a result, the number of legions involved in the wars increased considerably and the amount of supplies reaching the battlefront was limited only by the difficult mountain terrain and a bold enemy who lurked in every mountain gorge or valley. These wars can also be seen as a model for gaining (and using) profound knowledge of the terrain in northern Hispania. Good intelligence gathering and a strong leadership – especially embodied in Agrippa – served as a counter to the difficult conditions.

In the year 27, when Augustus had become the sole ruler of Rome, there were three regions in the north and northwest of Hispania that had not been brought under Roman control: Cantabria, Asturias and Gallaecia (Galicia). The wars that had broken in these regions in the year 26 were named after Cantabria. This is due to two main reasons: the first is that according to most of the sources, the Cantabrias led the revolts in the north. The second is that most writers did not really differentiate between the peoples, and called them all 'Cantabrians'. Everything known so far indicates that these peoples were not ethnic entities separated from the rest of the peoples in north and central Hispania. Once a 'mixture' was created following the invasion by Indo-European tribes, the ethnic and demographic differences between these tribes were not significant, despite certain cultural differences.

These wars have not received proper attention in historical research, and therefore the information we have about them is partial and fragmented, and based mainly on the works of Livius, Florus, Suetonius and Orosius.

The reasons for the wars are unclear; it is possible that they were initiated by Augustus – after finding the right reason, of course. This was part of his plan to rule 'from Cadiz to the Alba River'.

The Romans had been aware for quite some time that there were rich and very active gold mines in Hispania, and that these served as the basis for the jewellry industry. It is quite possible that Augustus considered the mines as a possible source of finance for his conquest and construction plans.

In the year 29, Plutarchus and Dio Cassius mention the Cantabrians as one of the peoples who caused problems in north Hispania; Florus indicates that the Cantabrians were the most belligerent of all the peoples in northern Hispania, and that they were interested not only in protecting their own freedom, but also to conquer more land by making unprovoked raids on neighboring settlements. Six victories of Roman magistrates are recorded between the years 36-26, and these indicate that there had been a state of war in the years preceding the 'official' war. This reinforces the argument for those who think Augustus had set out on a defensive war. It is important to note that according to Dio Cassius, Augustus was heading the military campaign to conquer Great Britain, but was forced to change his plans and supress the revolts in northern Hispania.

Maggie accepts Dio Cassius' view and claims that being a very practical person, Augustus preferred to be remembered as the one who had finally ended the Hispanic wars, rather then venture into the unknown Great Britain. If this is the case, then Augustus' conquest of north-west Hispania was not planned, but dictated by operational necessity. Suetonius said that these had been the only wars that Augustus had personally taken part in since he had risen to power. In the year 26, Augustus had begun moving north with an army of seven legions and auxiliary forces.[15] He advanced in a formation of three parallel rows along the narrow, winding mountain roads of Cantabria. In addition to his land forces, Augustus had a fleet of warships to blockade the enemy's coastal areas, thus cutting-off any escape routes.

Dio Cassius wrote that the Cantabrians and Asturians, although their forces were smaller than the Romans, knew the terrain and avoided large-scale battles as often as possible. Instead, they focused on making lightning raids from the mountains, followed by a rapid and organized retreat, i.e. guerrilla warfare.

At the beginning of the campaign the Romans had conquered Bergida, a main Cantabrian city. The Cantabrian and Asturian settlement model was based, at least since the fourth century, on fortified settlements located on top of hills which had provided good defence against invasions from Europe. These settlements also preserved the people's separatist culture for centuries: until the wars against the Romans.

The first major battle took place at Mons Vindius. To date, the mountain has not been identified, and researchers still argue as to its exact geographic location. When the Cantabrians felt that they were at a disadvantage, they retreated into the mountains but were later forced, mainly due to hunger, to surrender.

The fighting became more ferocious. Disease spreading rats infested the camps of the Roman army and there was also a shortage of supplies. The local tribes used guerrilla tactics to attack Roman supply columns travelling from Gallia-Aquitania, in south-west Gaul, through the narrow gorges and valleys of the Pyrenees. The Romans were forced to negotiate with the local tribes for every supply convoy that was intended for the army. Disease began to spread in the Roman army, regardless of rank. Augustus himself became ill (or as Suetonius wrote: 'badly wounded in an accident') and was evacuated to Terraco.[16] When Augustus could no longer personally command his forces in the war, he handed over to the legate P. Carisius who led the army, marching in three rows, toward the northwest and into Asturian territory.

The Asturian soldiers were not intimidated by the advancing Roman forces, and positioned three formations to oppose them, one against each row. However, the Romans had received intelligence reports detailing these plans from local people who had betrayed the Asturians. Carisius brought in reinforcements from the south, and this saved the Romans from a crushing defeat and the failure of the entire operation. The Asturians were defeated and their capital city, Lancia, surrendered. It is thought that the coins bearing the name of Carisius were minted to commemorate this event.

With the surrender of the Cantabrians the region was calm until the year 25, when the Romans launched an attack on the last region in Hispania which was not under their control; Galicia in the northwest of the Iberian Peninsula. For this attack, the Romans advanced in a two-row formation: one commanded by C. Antistius Vetus, the governor of Hispania Citerior, and the other commanded by Carisius. The Galician soldiers were driven to the highest areas in their territory and took up positions inside a fortress at the top of Mons Medulius.

There is a controversy regarding the geographic location of this mountain, but it can be argued, with some certainty, that according to the works of Florus and etymologic parallels that it lay in the Sierra do Courel between present-day Lugo and Orense, Galicia.

The Romans laid siege to the fortress by building a wall, 29km in length, around the perimeter. They then sat and waited for a Galician surrender.

The fortress defenders who had no wish to be taken alive by the Romans, decided to take their own lives. Florus, who did not differentiate between the tribes of north Hispania and treated them all as the one people, described the event in somewhat romantic terms. He wrote that the barbarians who had never been under the control of others, considered their loss of freedom as a fate worse than death. Florus added that they committed suicide by using swords and fire, while at a celebratory banquet.

Following his triumph, Augustus declared that all of Hispania had been conquered and that it had been a successful military campaign. He returned triumphant to Rome. There he ordered the building of Iovis Tonantis, a temple to Jupiter, as a token of his gratitude to the god for his speedy recovery from the illness he had contracted in Hispania.

Augustus even ordered the closure of the temple to the god Ianus, to symbolize that the entire empire is at peace, a peace brought by him.

In addition, he built the *Ara Pacis* (altar of peace) to commemorate his triumph. The altar, which was erected in the field of Mars and completed in the year 9, was dedicated to Augustus by the Senate to commemorate his double victory – Hispania and Gaul.

The quiet period did not last for very long in northern Hispania. It seems that immediately following the return of Augustus to Rome, the unrest began again. In the years 24, 22, 19 and 16, there had been large-scale revolts mainly amongst the Asturians and Cantarians; these were probably caused by the iron fist policy employed against them by the

Roman governors. The revolt in the year 19 was the fiercest, and Augustus sent Marcus Vipsanius Agrippa, his right-hand man, to command the army to confront the rebels.

On his arrival in northern Hispania, Agrippa had first to deal with the demoralized state of the army. The living conditions in the field were harsh and many soldiers were afraid to fight against the Cantabrians and refused to even make contact with the enemy. Agrippa had three legions at his disposal: the sixth legion 'VI Vitrix', the seventh 'VII Gemina'and the tenth 'X Gemina'. At the end of the war, these legions would play an important role in the integration of Roman culture into northern Hispania. They played a role in the founding of the city of Caesar-Augusta (Saragossa) in Hispania Terraconensis, which was built on the ruins of Salduba, capital of the Edetani region.

Since the Cantabrians, who were entrenched in the mountains, had knowledge of Roman military tactics, they managed to delay their progress. However, after many weeks of Sisyphean work employing both force and diplomacy, Agrippa was victorious.

When the fighting was over, Agrippa decided to allow the survivors to settle in villages in the lower regions and granted them land. The reasonable explanation for this is that if more revolts should occur, then the situation would be easier for the Roman army to control. Once the conquest of Hispania had been completed, Augustus rearranged the provinces: Hispania Ulterior was divided into Baetica (Andalucia), and Lusitania, which included present-day Portugal, in addition to the areas that had been previously conquered in the northwest. Pliny the Elder wrote that according to Agrippa, Lusitania covered an area 370km long and 360km wide. At a later time, Augustus transferred the last regions to be conquered, though still not peaceful, to Hispania Citerior. As a contingency in the province, he retained the only legion that remained in all of Hispania on a permanent basis. Augustus transferred Baetica, the peaceful and most 'Roman' of the three provinces, to the control of the Senate. Filled with satisfaction and pride, Augustus noted in the Res Gestae that he returned to Rome all the banners and standards that other Roman commanders-in-chief had lost when defeated.[17] He also wrote that he had founded several soldier colonies in Hispania, probably for those who had been released from the army at the end of the Cantabrian wars. An inscribed copper table, dating to the year 15, was discovered at El Bierzo in the border area between Asturia and Galicia. It attests to a line of administrative reforms introduced following the new division of territory. The inscription names a province located 'north of the Transduerian' [river Douro] which did not previously exist. It possibly disappeared when these areas were unified under Hispania Citerior.

In order to expediate the process of integrating Roman culture into Hispania – and also in order to control the region more efficiently – Augustus began building an immense system of roads throughout the Iberian Peninsula. The new roads connected Hispania through the Pyrenees to the south of Gaul. Additional roads encompassed the country and many were built along the Mediterrenean and Atlantic coasts, others connected north-west Hispania to the rest of the Iberian Peninsula. Augustus founded strategically placed new cities, such as Asturica Augusta, built at the heart of the area conquered during the wars in the northwest; and Emerita (Merida), on the banks of the Guadiana, built by and for veteran soldiers just released from military service. Over the years, Emerita had become the capital of the province of Lusitania.

By the time Augustus and Agrippa defeated the north-west regions of the península, it had taken 200 years to conquer Hispania. The process, which had begun at the end of the third century with the Second Punic War (known as the annexation of Hispania to the Roman Empire) was long and painful. Many key people in the history of the Roman Republic had gained an eternal reputation from their involvement in Hispania, such as Scipio 'Africanus', Cato, Scipio Aemilianus, Pompeius and others. The wars had changed the structure and components of the Roman army considerably, which is the subject of the discussion in the following chapters.

Chapter Three

The Limits of Power:

Rome and the Limitations of Fighting Distant Wars

Internal politics as a catalyst or curb to wars

Roman internal politics had largely dictated the events in Hispania. The complex relations between the families who ruled the Roman Senate and their wish to retain control of government had prevented, to a large extent, the creation of a broad senior level of command in the army. This indirectly limited the ability of the army to defeat the enemy. As a result, commanders in Hispania were forced to sign agreements with the local chieftains and settle for indirect control of the area.

There are two schools of research regarding the reasons for the exceptional expansion by Rome in the second century. I will present them in this chapter and explain why one is much preferable.

Several centuries earlier, Rome was an unknown city in the Latium region, and was subject to the Etruscans. In the course of the second century, this unknown city had been transformed into the largest and most powerful empire in the Mediterranean. This is an undisputed fact in historical research. However, when the question of how the Romans achieved this impressive status is asked, opinions become varied and divided. As Beard and Crawford state, there are two main schools of thought concerning the impressive territorial expansion of the Roman Republic throughout the Mediterranean Basin in the third to first centuries, as well as conquering the kingdoms that had ruled for many years.

Researchers such as Badian, Campbell, Millar, Scullard, Sherwin-White and many others, represent the most popular school of thought.

These researchers claim that Rome had operated, in the main, on the basis of self-defence. Campbell claims that the 'strategy and long-term planning were only secondary to greed and the power aspiration (of the senators)'.

Other peoples such as the Gaul and Germanic tribes in northern Italy, or leaders such as King Pyrrhus or Hannibal in the south and west are those who attacked Rome, and sometimes even threatened the existence of the Republic. Therefore, Rome had no choice but to defend itself and fight the aggressors. Reference to this is found in Cicero's words: 'the only reason in going to war is in hopes of eventually securing long-term peace in the future.' A series of unplanned wars over the decades and centuries had led Rome to, unintentionally, conquer vast territories. At the end of a very long period it controlled a vast empire that stretched throughout the Mediterranean Basin and included most of the Hellenistic world and beyond.

This school of thought can be reasonably used to explain another question which arises from the study of the Roman conquest during those centuries in regard to the avoidance of the annexation of vast territories. Badian claims that this is simply a matter of sophistication on the part of Rome thus enabling it to avoid the annexation of areas, beyond the shores of the Apennine Peninsula, which it had fought for and won. Badian believes that Rome acted according to the principles of *utile* (profitability) and *honestum* (morality) and succeeded throughout the second century to restrain a natural instinct to translate military success into vast conquest. Badian defines this policy by quoting Mommsen: 'The second century was characterized by the sophisticated policy of refraining from annexing territories…' This is how Rome operated in the year 168, by refraining from conquering areas in the Balkans until the third Macedonian War against King Perseus (at the end of which Macedonia was annexed) in order to prevent another war.

North Africa was annexed only in the year 146, after the destruction of Carthage at the end of the Third Punic War, and the centre of the Carthaginian area had become a new province by the name of Africa.

Hispania is an exception in this regard. In spite of an agreement signed between Rome and Carthage in the year 201 to end the Second Punic War – an agreement that revokes any chance of Carthaginian return to Hispania – Rome did not leave Hispania, but instead launched a long military campaign to complete the conquest.

Badian specifies three main reasons for the Senate's policy of refraining from annexation from the third century until mid-second century. The first reason is a practical one: the Romans operated across the sea in territories which were in a state of constant war. These wars were very expensive and demanded costly manpower from Roman citizens and allies. Therefore, the Senate believed that in an equation of cost versus benefit, the annexation or even permanent presence of Roman soldiers in these areas was not worthwhile.

The second reason according to Badian was the reaction of Roman nobility, in the first half of the second century, on receiving an *imperium* which demanded a great responsibility overseas, especially in the west. The example of the Scipio brothers, whose failure in Hispania had led to their death at the beginning of the Second Punic War was still fresh in the memory of these nobles, who thought that the risks outweighed the benefits.

The third reason that Badian mentions is the abhorrence felt in Rome when they learned of the disgraceful behaviour of many of the Roman elite who had been sent to serve as officers in Hispania. Actually, it should be noted that this did not stop the Senate – in a typical display of double standards – from returning Mancinus, the most maligned of its agents, to public life. In the year 137, during the Celtiberian War, Mancinus found himself ambushed and surrounded by thousands of Celtiberian soldiers, and had no choice other than to surrender in order to save his army from death or slavery. The Senate in Rome had refused to acknowledge the treaties signed between Mancinus and the Celtiberian leaders, since these were considered disgraceful for the Roman Republic. Mancinus had asked the Senate to show him the same grace they had shown to C. Pompeius three years earlier, but he lacked the strong support that Pompeius enjoyed in the Senate. The senators decided to send Mancinus back to the Numantines as a gift.

Another case related to *magistratus* S. Galba, who was saved from a death penalty in spite of his unsuccessful military service in Hispania. In the year 149, Cato, who had served as a censor in the Senate attacked Galba over his failures when serving in Hispania. Fluvius Nobilior, another failed veteran of the Hispanic wars, came to his defence.

Mancinus returned to Rome, after being humiliated in Hispania and in Rome, and was given back his revoked citizenship. He then rose through the clerical ranks until he was awarded the status of a *praetor* once again. It seems that the Senate found it difficult, perhaps even impossible, to punish one of their 'own' as they would a commoner.

Some say that the refusal by the Senate to acknowledge the treaties with the Hispanic peoples resulted, according to Frank, from a policy that made the Romans 'play' on their own terms with the enemy who was 'known' to be unreliable and even for treacherous behavior: a form of 'give as good as you get' retaliation. I cannot negate this view, but referring to it as a deciding factor in the decisions made by the Senate is fanciful. When this view is expanded, one naturally arrives at the head of the pinnacle of the Roman Republic – the Senate. If we continue the same line of thought, we will arrive at the conclusion that Roman Senate had opposed the establishment of new provinces in order to satisfy the ruling elite.

Several families, ten to twenty, from the Roman *nobilitas* (nobility) wanted to preserve their exclusivity in the highest echelons of the Republic, the consulate and *praetoriate*. At the end of the third century, six of Rome's noble families had led the Senate and set the political agenda. Those included the Fabii, Claudii, Cornelii, Aemilii, Valerii, and the Scipionii in particular. Out of the 108 consuls elected between 146 and 200, only eight did not belong to these families.[18] It is likely that the 'oligarchs' feared that numerous wars and their outcome, namely the victories, would lead to the addition of new territories to the Roman Empire. In this case, the question was who would head the different armies that Rome would be forced to assemble, and who would be the governors for the new provinces. Roman nobility had no way to handle, in terms of numbers, the situation of multiple command tasks. It is quite possible that instability in Hispania and the continuous exhaustion of resources had led to this type of thinking.

Also, it was common knowledge that there was no need to be physically, militarily or politically present in order to control remote territories. It was possible to create a situation of remote control to ostensibly preserve the independence of the different peoples, and at the same time save Rome from encountering challenging situations in distant places.

This was done through the signing of treaties. Rome employed this method many times in its dealings with the Hellenistic world. Each of the signing parties was aware of its position according to Roman *amicitia*, which was completely different from the *philia* in the Hellenistic world. In the third century, when Rome regularized its relations with the Greek-Iberian city of Saguntum, it had used this type of agreement as a legislative basis (and an excuse) to declare war on Hannibal.

As in any oligarchy, whether in ancient or modern times, the ruling families aspired to maintain their power and this aspiration was a crucial factor in policy making. The Roman nobles did not wish to increase the number of high-ranking positions which entitled their holders to an *imperium*. This would mean creating an opening for 'new people' and losing a share of the government which had been exclusively theirs. Indeed, no new positions were added, apart from two *praetors* (there had been four until then), and two out of the six *praetors* were to serve in the city of Rome.

Therefore the question arises: why had the Senate supported most of the wars that Rome was involved in, and very often urged the fighting to continue until the enemy unconditionally surrendered. Occasionally this was done contrary to the opinions of the commanders in the field.

In spite of the difficulties in recruiting soldiers and because of additional financial problems and the over-deployment of forces, especially between the years 151 and 138, the Senate annulled agreements signed in Hispania between Roman commanders and the local tribes. The result was that the commanders were forced to continue fighting until a final victory and unconditional surrender. During the first and second centuries, this became the only acceptable ending to most Roman wars in Hispania.

An example can be found on the *Tabula Alcantarensis* copper tablet. The inscription, which was engraved in 111-112, describes the unconditional surrender of a Hispanic people (whose name has been worn away) and was presented to Lucius Caesius, the Roman commander.

Richardson claims that the main reason for Rome's inflexible stance is that the trauma of the war with Hannibal had become etched into the Roman psyche, forming a state of mind according to which Rome must not provide the enemy with a chance to recover and threaten again: therefore the enemy should be defeated and annihilated.

For example, in the case of Carthage the Romans made an exception from their policy to avoid direct control of remote territories – after the First Punic War and in the period between the Hispanic wars and following the Second Punic War – and annexed the territories that they conquered from Carthage, including Sicily, Sardinia and Corsica.

In addition, Richardson considers the personality of Scipio Aemilianus and his power in the Senate as another reason for the decision to destroy Numantia and Carthage and annex any new territories.

Harris and Lutwak represent the second school of thought among others. Lutwak claims that the Roman conquests (although he only writes about the period of the *Principate*) are a result of pre-meditated planning. Harris claims that the conquests resulted mainly from wars that Rome had initiated, and the reason for these wars was the wish of the ruling families in Rome to earn money and gain glory. Harris believes that the Senate, which was the centre of power for these families, intended to 'provide' wars and create opportunities for them to realize their objectives. Therefore, the Senate came up with a plan for gradual expansion. The very few periods of peace between the wars occurred due to internal problems in Rome, such as the difficulty of recruiting soldiers, or over-exploiting the limits of the state treasury.

The critics of this school of thought argue that Harris was wrong in assuming that the Senate had operated as an autonomous body and that it had been continuously controlled for decades, if not centuries, by those high-nobility families. Sherwin-White reminds us that there were 300 people in the Senate, and around half of them had no real chance of advancing beyond the position of a *quaestor*. Therefore, he claims, that it is not very likely that they had been over-motivated to venture into unnecessary wars: consequently, the argument of the Harris school is unfounded. Campbell says that the rivalries between the high-nobility families that controlled the Senate very often acted as a restraint to the conquest. Each family was afraid of the power that a rival family might gain as a result of a victory. The critics of Harris' theory think that it is also contrived in terms of the *praetors*: a person who has just been elected as a *praetor* was likely to be sent without an army to a peaceful province that did not border on another, such as Sardinia or Sicily, and not to an area in which the army was active such as Hispania, Macedonia or Asia. Therefore, the appointment as a *praetor* did not guarantee a rise through the ranks of government, nor was it a way of obtaining wealth.

In the second half of the second century, the policy of non-annexation had undergone changes, particularly in the Hellenistic east. Scullard points out that the increase in the number of maritime merchants mainly in Italy, and of wealthy people in general, had led to their increased influence over government institutions in Rome. He indicates that this is one of the main factors that had caused the change in their approach to the annexation of new territories in the eastern Mediterranean.

The Italian merchants wanted their competitors, especially the Greek, to disappear from the eastern Mediterranean waters. Direct control by Rome over the Aegean Sea and the coast would provide those merchants with a monopoly over rich markets in that area. It is likely that the existence of the many gold and silver mines in Hispania, which were exceptionally large and produced high-quality ore, had led to a similar decision.

When summing up and examining the arguments of the two schools of thought, it seems to the author that it is very difficult to defend a theory that maintains that the sons of a few families in the Roman Senate produced a master plan for a comprehensive conquest. Rostovtzeff wrote that in the second century, Roman patriotism had reduced while personal interests – including family interests – had grown stronger. Significant amounts of evidence concerning the conflicts between these families – according to the school of 'planned conquests' they were supposed to work in co-operation – only reinforce this argument.

An example is the case of Quintus Servilius Caepio, a consul in the years 141-140, who was behind the faction that was opposed to the agreement Quintus Pompeius Aulus had signed with the Numantines. This was because Caepio had been adopted by the Fabii family and was a friend of Scipio Aemilianus, the political rival of Aulus.

There is also evidence of families that belonged to opposing factions in the Senate continuing to differ even when there was a real danger to the very existence of Rome.

Therefore, these family groups cannot be considered as a closed and unified body which made long-term plans. The high nobility were probably an 'appointments committee' for *imperium*-related positions, in order to avoid conflict among themselves and to prevent new people from entering the centre of the Roman government. In reality, there was no need for conspiracies or long-term planning so that only 'our people' would be in power. The method – which existed in the 'civilized Roman Republic' of the second century, and at least until the murder of T. Gracchus in the year 133 – according to which the Senate was the one to actually determine the results of the elections prevented this.

Either way, in the course of the second century there had been many wars in different areas from the Iberian Peninsula to Mesopotamia; wars that usually ended in a Roman victory and the addition of vast new territories to the Roman Empire.

The need to rule these territories had brought about many dramatic changes in the Republic, mostly due to disagreements among those who governed. These changes eventually led in the year 27, to the replacement of the republican regime with a sole ruler (Emperor). The Senate and the noble families would play a minor role.

Limitations of the army commanders' *Imperium*

The republican system of government was no longer suitable for the needs of Rome, and this was clearly manifested in the many deficiencies of the army's high command: the lack of senior commanders. The number of position holders, who were authorized – in the legislative terms of the existing government – to command the army, was much smaller than the requirements of an army that had to fight several simultaneous long wars in distant locations. The duration of the mandate these officers received to complete their military mission was suitable for the wars of the fifth to third centuries, but not the wars of the second century which required months of preperation to recruit and assemble an army for deployment to the battlefield.

The commanders, either a consul or *praetor*, did not receive sufficient soldiers or the time required to perform their duty in an adequate manner according to the requirements of the Senate and also Roman tradition. This was the reason for the many difficult situations which frequently confronted the Romans in Hispania. As previously mentioned, the families that controlled the Senate were looking for ways to fill vacant positions without bringing new people into the system. These attempts did not solve the problems and only postponed the end of the system to the next century.

It is rare to find throughout the history of the Roman Republic, long periods of time in which the Roman army was not involved in fighting at least one war. Until the 80s of the third century and the war against Pyrrhus, King of Epirus – especially until the beginning of the Second Punic War in 264 – Roman wars were conducted not far away from the metropolis and were usually fought during the summer months.

The Roman soldier who had been recruited for a defined military operation, marched with his unit to the battlefield, fought (if at all) for several months, then returned home to be released from military service and went back, as a citizen, to his family and work. The army was headed by one of two consuls, occasionally both, according to the operational requirements or political circumstances in Rome prevailing at the time. To quote Rich and Shipely: '...the summer marked the beginning of the war season for the consuls...'[19]

Due to the consequences of the First Punic War, the Romans were forced to make considerable changes to the traditional deployment of their army. They now had to station a permanent army in Sicily. For the first time in Roman history there was a need to build a large fleet of ships: this was to become a very complex task. This also required the recruitment of crews and instruction in how handle the ships and fight at sea. Navigators received lessons on the weather and winds, marine currents and sea conditions. When Sicily, and later Sardinia, became subject to Roman control, two more *praetors* were appointed to head each of the new provinces. These territories were close to the peninsula and the appointments were for one year, as was customary at the time.

The Second Punic War (218 to 201) posed a greater challenge for the government in political, social, economic and military terms. However, Scullard mentions that the Roman regime was built in such a way that it was possible to adapt if necessary to relatively large changes. In order to defend against Hannibal and attempt to defeat the Carthaginians, it was essential to build an army and fleet on a large scale and with great urgency. This required manpower and economic resources of such a magnitude that Rome had never previously needed. These extra resources were extremely expensive and the money required was not available.

New, mainly social, laws were required and these were enacted by Flaminius: this illustrates the ability of the system to make such changes and create a specific solution. This was an essential requirement for the Republican regime, which contributed greatly to the fact that it remained stable until the 30s of the second century and survived until the end of the first century.

Rome had suffered heavy losses in the Second Punic War, especially in the first years, making it necessary to begin a massive recruitment drive for soldiers. The battlefronts were remote and numerous: Hispania, South Gaul, North Africa, Sicily and Illyria. Very often, a garrison was required to deploy, at the same time, a large number of its soldiers to a different area, far from each other and even further from Rome. Several legions were set up especially for this war and it is known that at a certain period there were twelve legions on active service. All these legions required a commander, and there was no choice but to appoint more people other than the two consuls.

The legislative process of awarding an *imperium* to magistrates and position holders, who were awarded the authority of a *magistrate* (*pro-magistrate*), had begun to change in Hispania, with the arrival of the Scipio brothers. The tradition regarding the army's command structure in Hispania, which was customary in the Roman Republic at the end of the third century, determined that there should be a clear separation between the two domains: the legislative aspect and the strategic aspect. The certification to commanding positions and the definition of the policy were under the jurisdiction of the Senate. The second aspect was a military issue, and as such, it was the responsibility of the high commander in the field, usually the consul. In practice, a large number of the decisions, military and other, were made in the field by the army commander, in order to provide an immediate response to the challenges that arose during the war.

Members of the Senate in Rome could do nothing but agree with the decisions of the commander and approve them, as they often did. In some matters, such as the recruitment of soldiers and their transfer to Hispania, the commander in the field was indeed completely dependent on the Senate. Other matters, which were seemingly under the exclusive jurisdiction of the Senate, were handled by the commander in the field based on his discretion. For example, being dependent on receiving supplies from Rome very often dictated tactics in the Hispania campaign, so the commander-in-chief made his decision to source supplies locally.

The saga of the Roman conquest of Hispania had actually begun in the autumn of the year 218, when Cnaeus Scipio crossed the Pyrenees leading the consular army of Publius Scipio. P. Scipio awarded his brother the authority of an *imperium pro praetore* which the Senate was forced to approve.

In spite of an innate conservatism, the Roman Senate quickly adapted to the new geopolitical situation. Several years later, the Senate had demonstrated creativity and a rather developed sense of survival by appointing young Cornelius Scipio (the future 'Africanus') to a consul. C. Scipio received the *imperium pro consule* (consular authority) at the young age of 25, and managed to achieve the position of *Aedile* in the *cursus honorum* (honours rank).

The circumstances of the appointment of C. Scipio to the high position in Hispania were exceptional. It seems that the description of the appointment in later Greek and Roman sources (especially Polybius and Livius) was influenced by the description of the appointment of Scipio Aemilianus in 151. It is likely that the description provided by Polybius regarding the appointment of Aemilianus to a consul was transliterated from the case of Africanus, which preceded it by nearly six decades (Polybius took part in the journeys made by Aemilianus to Hispania and Carthage). As for Cornelius Scipio, Livius tells that the *Comitia Centuriata* (Centuriate Committee) had awarded Scipio an *imperium pro-consul*.

In order to help Scipio in his mission, or maybe to keep a watchful eye on him, the Senate also sent Junius Silanus, as a *pro-praetor*, a lower *imperium* than that awarded to C. Scipio.

In 206, when Scipio had completed his mission and left Hispania, the Senate was faced with a legislative problem regarding that country. How should they deal with the management of the new remote territory? Should they leave the area or remain? If they remained, how could they rule these areas?

The situation in Hispania was very difficult, they were to live among natives that Mommsen described as having 'different degrees of barbarism', very different to the ideal situation where the Phoenicians and civilized Romans lived side-by-side. There were no precedents in the history of the Roman Republic for such a situation.

Until the existing laws were replaced with laws which were more fitting to the new situation, a process of trial and error was required. And so, for years it had not been clear what the status of the new territory was and what authority the Roman commanders-in-chief that were sent there to govern, actually had. Sometimes the authority discussed was *imperium pro consul* and other times, it was *imperium pro praetor*.

The Senate, therefore, employed different legislative tricks to deal with the new military and administrative needs, without harming the painful issue of the Senators, i.e. without introducing 'new people' into the Republic's highest positions. In 198, the Senate added two additional *praetors* and their number increased from four to six. Until the civil wars of the mid-first century, the Romans had functioned with two *consules* and six *praetors*. Apart from adding two *praetors*, the Senate refrained from increasing the number of high positions. Instead, in order to meet the operational needs, the Senate used to extend the tenure of these positions.

Propagatio imperii (tenure extension) of magistrates holding an *imperium*, as was Scipio's case, was an unusual act at the beginning of the Second Punic war against the Carthaginians in Hispania (at the end of the third century and beginning of the second), and the approval was given *post factum*.

However, in the course of the second century, it became the norm. This norm was probably implemented also in junior positions, those inferior than *consul* or *praetor*. In an inscription from the first century found in Carthago Nova, appears the name of a magistrate named Q. Cassius Longinus. The inscription says that Longinus was awarded the title of *Quaestor pro-praetor*. These superior follow-up roles were previously served by *praetors*, and the Senate was the one to extend the tenure of the commanders.

From the second century onwards, the *pro-praetors* and *pro-consules* were appointed in order to serve in the provinces. Between the years 143 and 134, during the Numantine war in Hispania, one of the two province governors was always a consul and the other a pro-consul.

The increase in the number and importance of the *praetors* in the first half of the second century was expressed also in the high number of the victory processions held in their honour: eighteen victory processions between 200 and 167, as opposed to only one in the third century (in the year 241), and none in the previous centuries. In the second century, several victory processions were held in honour of *privati* (citizens), holders of *privati cum imperium* (citizen authorities).

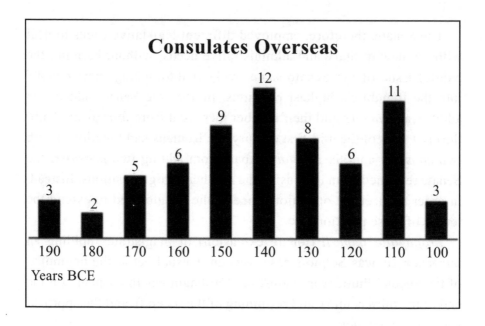

In the second half of the second century, however, there had been a significant decrease in the number of cases in which *praetors* commanded a Roman army in any battle. This was due to two main reasons.

Firstly, although Rome had fought in several large-scale wars (the Third Punic War, the Numantime war, the conquest of Greece, etc), there had been a decrease in the number of simultaneous wars. In addition, the method of assigning the consuls had changed.

As opposed to the first half of the century in which the consuls had fought mainly in northern Italy – the most important war zone for Rome due to its proximity to the capital – from then on, the consuls were sent to fight wars in a few remote and more prestigious places such as Macedonia, Greece and Asia Minor.

This meant that two consuls had the chance to command the army during those years, and they were given the opportunity to attain the desired military glory. Between the years 153 and 133, the fierce fighting in Hispania had led to the permanent presence of one of the consuls, and in effect, most of the opportunities for gaining triumph and victory were presented to the consuls and not *praetors*, who had fewer authorities than the former.

As previously mentioned, Rome's victories at the end of the third century and the first half of the second century, in the Second Punic War, and the wars in the East against the Hellenistic, Macedonian and Seleucid kingdoms, had led to Rome controlling vast territories far away from the centre of government: Hispania, Greece, Macedonia, many islands (in the east and west of the Mediterranean) and Asia Minor. In most of these areas, Rome was forced to assign several permanent legions.

This situation had led to an increasing independence for the officers in the field, leading to virtual autonomy, although perhaps not always *de jure*, but at least *de facto*. This was especially apparent in Hispania. At the beginning of the second century, Cato had begun decreasing the dependency of his army upon Rome, in terms of supplies. He preferred to supply most of his army's needs from the local agricultural produce, which was abundant and accessible, instead of being dependent on the mercy of the government in Rome. This was due to the fact that the Senate did not always agree with an officer on the situation and the requirements in the field. Also the shipment of supplies was dependent to a large extent on weather and sea conditions in the Mediterranean.

It often occurred that the *consule* or *praetors* commanding the Roman armies in Hispania made important decisions regarding whether to go to war or sign peace treaties with the different tribes. Very often, the Senate – although at the height of its power in the second century and able to intervene with the actions of the consuls – had acted as a 'rubber stamp' and approved *post factum* the actions of these commanders, specifically in relation to the treaties.

However, the Senate did occasionally intervene in the events in Hispania, and even down to the minutest detail. In the year 171, representatives of the Hispanic peoples had arrived in Rome to complain about the heavy economic burden imposed by the governors. The Senate decided to reverse the governors' decision, and return to the taxation system originally used in Hispania based on T. Gracchus' agreement from 179, which allowed the local people to collect the taxes.

Another example of the Senate's intervention in Hispania relates to the negotiations with the city of Segeda in the year 154. Appianus wrote that the peace that S. Gracchus had achieved was signed between him and the tribes, and the Senate played no part and did not even ratify the agreement afterwards. Livius differs in his version of the agreements between S. Gracchus and those signed between the Senate (with the tribes).

The Senate had mostly shown little interest in the course of the war in Hispania: as long as the ending was satisfactory for the senators. The Senate had no choice but to take this course of action, mainly due to it being dependent on the reports of commanders-in-chief in the field and its own inability to gather intelligence information. However, the authority to conduct a victory procession for the commander who had returned triumphant to Rome – or deny him the procession – was still in the hands of the Senate, and the commanders were well aware of this fact, and this could influence their judgment.

The extensive autonomy that the commanders enjoyed in Hispania had led to irregularities in the management of the provinces and also to acts of corruption. The commanders had been criticized more than once and many had said that their greed had been their major reason to declare war – a war financed by the state. The consul L. Lucullus was accused that he had declared war on the Vaccei tribe in the year 151, only because he wanted to obtain booty. According to Appianus, Lucullus had been driven by his desire for wealth and glory and had violated a peace treaty signed by Rome – behaviour which was inappropriate for a Roman noble – and would do again when launching difficult wars which were grossly expensive for the state treasury. After the Romans had won the battle at the outskirts of Cauca, the people of the village accepted the terms of surrender that he dictated: they paid him a considerable sum of money and surrendered many of the people as hostages and agreed to allow Roman forces entry to the village. However, Lucullus ordered all the men to be slaughtered and the city plundered.[20]

The case of Lucullus was by no means unique. Sulpicius Galba, the second consul in Hispania in that year, had betrayed and massacred the Lusitanians. That massacre had become the symbol of Roman cruelty and led to the Lusitanian revolt led by Viriathus.

Another example of inappropriate behaviour is that of M. Aemilius Lepidus Porcina, a pro-consul in Hispania Citerior. In the year 136, he declared war again against the Vaccei tribe by ignoring a specific order from the Senate in Rome. The war ended with a failure: Porcina lost his mandate and was returned to Rome in disgrace.

The three incidents described above led to a furious response from the Senate that had strongly condemned these commanders and took disciplinary measures against them. However, the three managed to survive this awkward situation and even return to political life. In this context it should be mentioned that the disgraceful behaviour of many commanders in Hispania had led to the shattering of the aura of integrity and justice in all that related to the conduct of the Roman government in the provinces. Richardson believes that the extensive autonomy that the commanders enjoyed in Hispania, together with the lack of interest in the detail of events, that Senate had usually shown, were the central factors that dictated Roman expansion in Hispania. He believes that this had been an area where it was possible to fight against an inferior enemy using asymmetrical fighting techniques, and at the same time, gain much booty and glory.

Rich does not completely negate this approach, but he does not agree with the claim that the ambitiousness of the commanders in the field was the main reason for the conquest. He indicates that most of the wars in Hispania in the second century had taken place in areas that had already been under Roman control; whereas the wars outside Roman-occupied areas were intended to ensure the security of the provinces, and were not part of an expansive tendency. Rich also relies on the fact that during that century, peace prevailed for relatively long periods of time.

Astin claims that the only way available to the Romans – if they wanted to avoid long endless wars with the different tribes in Hispania, especially the Celtiberians and Lusitanians – was to relinquish complete Roman control and settle for partial control. As far as the Senate was concerned, this was inconceivable, and it is likely that the Roman people held a similar view. The official Roman policy was to constantly strive for an absolute and final victory and unconditional surrender.

When detailing the major reasons for the multiplicity of wars in Hispania in the second century, we immediately think of two main reasons, namely the mountainous topography of Hispania and a persistent and very motivated enemy who knew the terrain extremely well and employed guerrilla-warfare tactics. The combination of these two factors had made it very difficult for the large, powerful and organized Roman army to demonstrate its might on the battlefield. But it is impossible to overlook the link between an officer's pursuit of wealth and military glory and a requirement to agree an unconditional surrender; the Senate refrained from *post factum* approval of non-combat agreements signed by the commanders in the field and could have prevented the continuation of the wars.

Mobilization of the fighting forces

The numerous wars that had taken place during the Second Punic War pushed the Roman mobilization system to its limits. Previously, the consuls would recruit two legions each before a 'seasonal war'. This was replaced by a new reality which required massive recruitment of forces which were then sent to different places and sometimes for several years. Roman citizens were recruited as soldiers; many were farmers or others who worked on the land and in the countryside.

Over time, the numerous recruitment drives began to endanger the economic strength of the entire country. Since the economy was based on agriculture, if an experienced farmer was absent for many years, it would be difficult to find a suitable replacement to work the land efficiently. The prospect of a financial profit as a result of the spoils of war did not compensate for the heavy burden imposed on citizens: certainly it did not encourage them to join the army.

The need for assembling more legions and better training for the soldiers was one of the main reasons for founding permanent legions and the beginning of the formation of a professional army. This process would continue long into the first century. As noted in Chapter 5, it was G. Marius who significantly boosted the process of change that the Roman army had undergone by making new laws.

The longest and hardest wars in the second century took place in Hispania, and so, this is the first place where permanent legions were stationed, outside of Rome and Sicily. These wars had also made it harder to recruit officers from the elite class. The stories told by veterans who had returned from Hispania, frightened Rome and the sons of good families tried to evade military service. The enemy was very powerful and the chance of returning home alive, rich and a hero – based on the common expectations – was almost zero.

Military service was a civil duty in Rome at the time of the Republic and *Principate*, at least until the third century AD. At the time of the Republic, the Senate was in charge of recruitment, while during the *Principate*, the *imperator* was the person in charge of this task. Anyone who evaded military service was severely punished by law, as much evidence in the sources proves. For example in the year 209, the social status of many people from the equestrian order who evaded, or attempted to evade military service was revoked. Cicero's view was quite strict, as he maintained that it would be impossible to sell evaders into slavery, since their behaviour had already proven that they were not free men. Augustus sold a citizen of the equestrian order into slavery along with all of his property, because he had 'arranged' for his sons to receive inadequacy certificates in order to be exempt from military service.

Military service was theoretically open only to Roman citizens. Allies could volunteer for the auxiliary forces, but it was strictly forbidden to recruit slaves into the army. In the second century AD, Emperor Trajan opened an investigation into the circumstances by which two slaves were conscripted into the army by using trickery. Trajan wrote to Pliny the Younger, ordering that the slaves should be brought to justice as well as the conscription officer if it was proven that he was negligent.

Military service was compulsory for all Roman citizens: those residing in the city of Rome, on the Apennine Peninsula and beyond throughout the Roman world.

Military service was an integral part of the life of every Roman citizen. Serving in the army was as natural as working, getting married or having children. The popular view in research maintains that significant numbers of citizens volunteered – at least until the first half of the second century – but conscription was considered a duty, and it was clear to all that evading military service would lead to harsh consequences. This can be deduced from the Latin term for conscription, '*dilectus*', which means 'an action that must be done'. In difficult times, as in the Second Punic War (218 to 201), or during the Numantine wars in the mid-second century in particular, the spirit of voluntarily serving in the Republic had declined. The need – actually the necessity – arose to enforce the 'law of compulsory conscription' more stringently.

It is quite possible that the expectation of receiving a reward, monetary or other for the service, had played an important role in the Roman 'spirit of volunteering to serve in the army'. It was customary for the officer to distribute rewards, especially lands, to his soldiers following a successful military campaign that resulted in the conquest of a vast and relatively rich territory. Scipio Africanus had done exactly that in the year 200, when he distributed plots of land to his soldiers who served under him in Africa, Sicily and Hispania. The size and quality of the land was directly proportional to the duration of service, as well as the military and social status.

The expectation of a substantial monetary reward, whether as a result of plundering or distribution of booty by the officer, had frequently constituted a very important factor in the Roman citizens' desire to serve in the army, and this also applied to the military service in Hispania. This also had an impact in the beginning of the third century, especially during the wars in the Hellenistic East, which were considered as having great potential for spoils of war.

Many citizens did volunteer for additional military service, but most of the conscription was made by enforcement of law. During the war with Hannibal, more than a quarter of the citizens of Rome were enlisted for reserve duty; not for a period of several months, but probably for years. From the second century on, there is an increase in the number of pieces of evidence expressing the citizens' dissatisfaction with the ever-growing burden of the lengthy military service.

As previously mentioned, the multiplicity of wars in the period between the Second Punic War until well into the second century, had led to the collapse of the conscription. These wars dwindled Rome's resources, both human and economic. Those who suffered most were naturally the people from the middle classes, who served as ordinary soldiers, and this was the group from which Rome recruited most of their soldiers.

The difficulty in recruiting sufficient soldiers to meet the army's requirements had led to the need for a different type of volunteer. A classic example is the case of the soldiers who survived the battle of Cannae: they had been recruited into the army between 216 and 214, fought, were defeated and barely survived that battle. They then continued to serve in Sicily and North Africa until the end of the Second Punic War and the final surrender of Carthage in 202. In this context, we can agree with Sabin, who writes that no defeat, as hard as it might be, will decide a war if the defeated side has the resources required to mobilize fresh forces and the desire to go on fighting.

In the year 200, the consul Sulpicius Galba received approval from the Senate to re-enlist soldiers from among Scipio Africanus' veterans to his military campaign in Hispania; some 2,000 enlisted. In 198, Flaminius was forced to re-enlist veterans of Africanus' army to serve in Hispania, only this time, most of them did not volunteer but were forced to return to active duty. In the 80s of the second century, soldiers who had completed their military service in Hispania were forced, many times, to wait a long time for their release due to the difficulty in finding replacements.

Scipio Aemilianus had no trouble in recruiting soldiers for his war against Carthage. Quite to the contrary due to the fact that this war had a huge potential for accumulating rich plunder (as well as a relatively easy victory). The aura of a victory for Scipio Aemilianus undoubtedly helped him to recruit 4,000 volunteers to go to Hispania and besiege the city of Numantia in the year 137, despite the fact that the prospect of a financial gain was much lower than that of Carthage.

The result was that many soldiers served in the army for most of their adult lives. One such soldier was Sempronius Ligustinus, a centurion since 198, who was recruited for the war in Macedonia in 200. After his release, he volunteered to go to Hispania under the command of Cato. He then served intermittently for several more years until he was finally released after twenty-two years military service. Another phenomenon discovered in the sources is the number of attempts to evade military service by the higher classes of Roman society.

Hispania was an unpopular battlefront, the fighting was hard, the wars were endless, and the possibility of gaining some 'serious' booty was very slim in comparison to the chances for those who fought in the east. In the middle of the second century, when the Celtiberian war broke out, the level of recruitment to the war in Hispania had reached an all-time low. The events that took place during the conscription of the year 151 serve as a testimony. Polybius tells of the endless battles and the high number of losses in the Hispanic Wars had spread terror among the young people of the Roman upper social class, much to the concern of the Senate elders. As a result, there were no suitable candidates for command positions. Only when Scipio Aemilianus showed his willingness to volunteer and command the army, did the rate of recruitment show a slight increase.

People from the upper social class who wanted to evade military service had more possibilities of doing so than the common people. The ever-decreasing number of cavalry soldiers who served in the Roman army attest to that.

As a lesson of the conscription crisis of 151, the Senate tried to regulate the problem of retirement for conscripts in the different locations. The problem was very difficult: those who served for a short period in Rome, Sicily and the other 'more tranquil' provinces or territories closer to home, and those who had served in the distant parts for long periods.

The Senate attempted to take the edge off this problem in many ways. They reduced the size of the forces serving in Hispania on a regular basis, as often as possible and at any given opportunity. It should be mentioned that the Roman force in Hispania was never large: each praetorian army included between 10,000 and 12,000 soldiers: very often two armies totalling 24,000 soldiers (together with the auxiliary forces and allies) were operating in the entire Iberian Peninsula. The Senate actually reduced by half the number of soldiers in Hispania: from two legions in each province (Hispania Citerior and Hispania Ulterior) to one in each province.

The reality in the field always had the final say, and in Hispania it was not always possible to plan for the long term. Every few years, it was necessary to operate a larger army than that permanently stationed in the peninsula and this was achieved by a massive reinforcement. The forces for this were selected by using a lottery method in order to decide which of the new recruits would serve relatively close to home, in Sicily, and those who were to serve in Hispania. At the request of Claudius Marcelus, the lottery took place for the first time in the year 152 and this was the only way that Lucullus was able to recruit a legion for his planned military campaign in Hispania.

In the year 137, the Senate prevented Scipio Aemilianus from carrying out another *supplementum* (mobilization of reserve forces) in addition to the usual mobilization in order to build an army strong enough to lay siege to and conquer the city of Numantia and bring an end to the war. In order to fill the ranks of his army, Aemilianus had to settle for recruiting volunteers.

One of the deterring issues for young Romans about to be conscripted, if not the most daunting one, was the duration of the military service. Until the beginning of the third century, the longest and hardest military service for a Roman soldier was in Gallia Cisalpina which lasted for one season, or one year at the most. However, in Hispania, this drastically changed and service often lasted several years. In addition, this was the first time that it was required to leave an army in both provinces on a regular basis. This was due to the time and distance from Rome, and also due to the many revolts which still plagued the region.

Number of legions active

There were other reasons to attempt the avoidance of military service. The chances of returning alive from Hispania were not very high, and the chance of returning with money was even slimmer. The

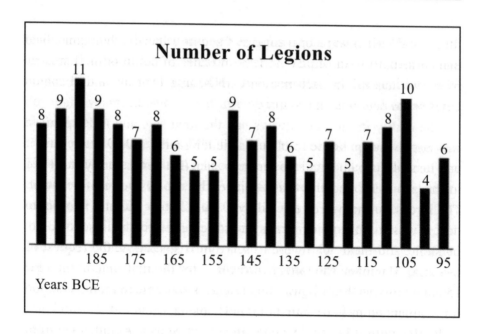

solution to the new situation was not clear-cut and it changed based on time and region. In some cases, as in 193 for example, soldiers in Hispania were released when the *supplementum* arrived. In 184, it was declared that soldiers who had served for a long time or those who proved exceptional bravery would be released and allowed to return to their homes.

For many the wording was vague, as it was not clear what the term 'long time' actually meant. In 180, soldiers in Hispania were released after six years service and there is evidence from the year 140 that this had become standard practice. Did they begin to limit the duration of service to six years in the year 180? Appianus does not provide a clear answer to this question.

What had been the size of the Roman army in the last three centuries of the Republic in general, and in Hispania in particular?

Livius provides many details concerning the number of legions, including auxiliary forces and *supplementa* (reserve forces) that were sent occasionally to bolster an army. However, are the figures that Livius had undoubtedly collected from the sources, precise? More importantly, did these legions always include the standard number of soldiers? It is probable that under normal conditions (which were quite rare), the numbers appearing in the sources truly reflect the reality in the field. However, this had not been the case during long and arduous wars, such as the Second Punic War or the Lusitanian and Numantine wars in Hispania.

In addition, there is no doubt that in the period following the disaster of the battle of Cannae, most of the Roman army units that had operated in Rome were below strength. According to the figures provided by Polybius, the four legions Scipio Africanus had brought with him to Hispania, in the first half of the second century, were not at full strength and he had to constantly rely on *supplementa* to fill the ranks of his army.

In the years 167 to 154, two legions were stationed in Hispania, one in each province. In the next four years, a consular army of two legions operated in Hispania Citerior and one legion in Hispania Ulterior. In the 40s of that century and despite the fact that in general there was a return to the standard of one legion for each province, the numbers changed from time-to-time due to the many revolts that took place in the Iberian Peninsula.

In the years 145 to 144, 142 and 133, a consular army was present in Hispania Ulterior, and in the years 143 to 142 and 133 it was in Hispania Citerior. This means that for several years there were five legions in all of Hispania (2½ times more than the standard that was defined for Hispania).

In the year 123, when C. Metellus fought against the pirates of the Balearic Islands, there were at least two legions in Hispania Citerior. At the beginning of the first century consular armies were in Hispania once again: during the years 98 to 92 or 91 in Hispania Citerior, and during 97 to 94 in Hispania Ulterior.

In the first century, the Senate ceased to be the sole authority regarding conscription. The great commanders-in-chief (Marius, Sulla, Pompeius, Crasus, Caesar and others) were to decide about all matters related to the war including the mobilization of the forces. The main reasons for building armies in the first century were the ambitions of the commanders to gain glory, wealth and power: not necessarily for the greater good of the Republic.

Throughout the Roman Empire the number of legions on active service had grown considerably. This massive growth, unprecedented in the Roman military history, did not forget Hispania. It was a central theatre in some of these wars: the revolt of Sertorius, the war between Julius Caesar and Pompeius, the war of the second triumvirate against the leaders of the Pompeius faction. Also the Cantabrian-Asturian wars: the only wars against external enemies. From the 80s of the first century until the completion of the conquest of north and northwest Hispania by Augustus and Agrippa, in the year 19, there had been between four and six legions positioned in Hispania on a regular basis.

Logistics and supply difficulties

The commanders of the Roman army were faced with many complex logistics challenges in the second century when fighting wars in distant lands. These challenges were associated mainly with the supplies sent from Rome by sea. The supply of provisions, produced in Rome and the surrounding farmland, on time and to the correct destination was not a simple operation. Another factor was a conflict of interests in Rome which had caused numerous delays in the shipment of supplies to the army in Hispania; or sending a smaller shipment than required contrary to the request of the officers in the field. The direct result was the beginning of the use of local resources to feed the Roman army.

Another process, which had probably begun at the end of the second century and ended with the reforms introduced by Marius, is the occasional use of panniers carried on the shoulders of the legionaire instead of on the back of a pack animal. Yet, despite all the complex logistical problems the Romans encountered in Hispania, their supply systems were still more developed and effective than those employed by the different tribes in the peninsula. This provided them with an additional advantage on the battlefield especially when there was a need for soldiers to recover after a fight.

Davies writes that the two main reasons for the supremacy of the Roman army were the skill of the soldiers and the quality of equipment. It is only reasonable to add a third reason: the logistic capabilities. The Romans were adept at sending military forces over large distances by land and sea and then keeping them supplied for long periods of time, giving them a serious advantage when beginning a war campaign. In modern research it is usual to consider Rome as a land-based superpower, yet it was the first to regularly use ships for the transportation of troops and supplies on a large scale. This allowed Rome not only to fight in wars abroad and conquer land, but also to support the continuous development of their vast empire. This was an ability that Hannibal lacked when invading the Apennine Peninsula.

The issue of supply is the main subject in any discussion concerning military logistics. The term 'supply' encompasses all the needs of an army on a campaign: clothing, food, money for the soldiers and officers, weapons, pack animals, raw materials and all other items related to the everyday life of a soldier. Le Bohec and other researchers of the Roman army use the term 'logistics' as a synonym for supply. For Goldsworthy and Roth, the word logistics in the context of the Roman army signifies both the supply and transportation.

The study of logistics in the ancient world in particular raises a few problems, including the lack of historical evidence. In ancient times, very little was written about logistics as it was considered to be uninteresting to the reader, and therefore to historians who had understood its nature but saw no reason to write on the subject. In addition, there was no meaningful message to be transferred for posterity. In this context, Luttwak wrote: '...most historians (of the ancient times) were aristocrats who have written for aristocrats'.

The resources that were at the disposal of the Roman Republic were quite large in comparison to those of other peoples. Sometimes these resources were not sufficient, and yet, to the enemy they seemed endless. The Second Punic War is an example. After each defeat in battle against Hannibal, Rome had managed to endure and even present another army, even stronger than the first. The truth is that this impression, on which rested the basis for Roman psychological deterrence, was not truly based on reality – quite to the contrary. The Roman army had become smaller, in comparison to the many theatres in which it had fought. Many times, the Senate or the commanders-in-chief had found it difficult to staff the smaller number of legions formed by Rome.

Rome had developed its resources and expanded them by using correct management and technical developments, especially in the area of transport. The Romans had built a network of roads and bridges on land and a merchant shipping fleet, which enabled them to move their resources with an unprecedented level of efficiency. Thus, Rome managed to build a vast empire and control it for hundreds of years, by using relatively small forces. This ability to open supply routes and defend them was of paramount importance to their military and administrative success in the last 200 years of the Republic and during the *Principate*. Roth notes: 'The success of the Roman army was dependent, very often, on bread, rather than iron.'

The Senate in Rome retained a tight control over all matters related to the army, especially sources of finance and supply. Occasionally in times of crisis, the Senate faced many difficulties when trying to provide for the needs of the army and was forced to seek creative solutions that would ensure continued operation. At the time of a severe financial crisis that occurred in the middle of the war against Hannibal, the Roman Senate turned to *societates publicanorum* (private bodies) requesting them to provide the supplies required by the army. In particular the army in Hispania and also those stationed in distant places.

In the year 215, Fluvius signed an agreement for the framework of a public tender, according to which he transferred the care for the supply to the Roman army in Hispania to three private companies. These and others had operated in Hispania for some twenty years, until the year 195, when Cato felt that he was capable of supplying the army and forced the companies out of the peninsula. Nevertheless, such companies continued to operate in Hispania, especially during periods of significant war. This explains why it is possible to read about the presence of the merchant representatives in the camp of Scipio Aemilianus during the siege of Numantia, some sixty years after they had been banished by Cato. Scipio Aemilianus banished the merchant representatives again, along with the prostitutes, soothe-sayers and other undesirable elements.

The Senate was responsible for appointing magistrates of military authority to fill the command positions (allocated by the Senate) in the provinces and other regions. Magistrates were awarded by the Senate among others, and given the authority to provide for the needs of their forces stationed in the province. But it was the Senate that controlled the State logistic system; the recruiting of manpower and finance and supply.

There were two types of military supplies: those that the army carried with it in the field and those that arrived from Rome. The Romans used two different terms to indicate the two types of supplies. Those that were transported by ship along with soldiers were 'initial supplies', called *impedimenta* which meant a train or convoy: some 1,400 donkeys and hundreds of chariots accompanied each legion: The second type of supplies was called *commeatus*.

The *impedimenta* were an integral part of the army and followed it everywhere. As in other armies this equipment was transported on chariots and pack animals, especially donkeys, and included a soldier's personal equipment and food. There were several differences between the Roman military transport network and that of other armies of the time: the fact that every legionnaire carried quite a heavy load of personal equipment on his back.

The Roman legionnaire was probably the first soldier in history to carry not only his personal equipment, but also additional equipment, which makes him almost similar to the modern-day soldier than to the native warrior of that time. Every *contubernium* (eight legionnaires) received a donkey, which carried a tent, cooking utensils and personal equipment.

The Romans were capable of moving very rapidly in the field despite all the *impedimenta* that they had to carry. Appianus says that it took Julius Caesar only twenty-seven days to march from Rome to Hispania; despite the fact that his army was carrying heavy equipment. Even if the figure that Appianus indicates seems somewhat low, it remains a remarkable achievement. It is known that the Roman army had the means to renew *impedimenta*. Each legion included professional artisans who were responsible for this task. Most army camps had cooking facilities, potteries, and workshops for the production and repair of weapons and other equipment.

The soldiers in each *contubernium* cooked for themselves. This way, the legion and even the entire army could operate almost as a self-sufficient autonomy. The only missing elements were raw materials, food and wood.

The raw materials arrived usually through the supply lines. This was one of the difficult problems that limited the army's freedom of movement, especially one that operated so far away from home. The longer the distance from the source of supply, the larger the chances were that something would go wrong on the way to the destination. In Hispania, this was exceptionally critical. As early as the beginning of the third century, Roman commanders in Hispania had anticipated that it would be very difficult for them to operate in the field when being completely dependent on supplies from home.

Appianus considered the food consumed by the Roman army as the main cause of the deterioration in the health of soldiers in Hispania. He claimed that their food did not contain all the ingredients, such as wine, oil and salt, he considered as vital nutrition for the health of a soldier. As early as 205, prior to the establishment of the two provinces of Hispania, the Romans forced the local people to provide their army with clothing and 'wheat for six months'. Only several decades later, the Roman governors of Hispania officially commenced the regular collection of taxes. Cato claimed at the beginning of the second century that the 'war should feed itself'. By this he meant that the army should commandeer wheat and other essential provisions from local sources, instead of receiving them from Rome.[21]

The supplies from Rome were delivered by *publicani* or *socii* (private contractors): most were Italians and some acquired a dubious reputation.

It should be noted too that had the Roman army operating in Hispania managed to substantially reduce its dependence on Rome, it would still need to receive a significant portion of its requirements, mainly money, through the same seaborne and land supply channels.

The operation and protection of the supply lines posed a problem for the Roman army (like any other army). The army was dependent on these supply lines, as it preferred not to collect agricultural produce or to cut down trees when involved in a war.

At the time of the Republic, the Romans did not have a fleet of cargo ships, and employed civilian shipping contractors, mostly Italian, to transport their supplies. The supply convoys preferred to sail as close as possible to the shore although going around the shores of the Mediterranean could be very dangerous, the proximity to land instilled the seafarers with a sense of security. These convoys would transport all the goods necessary for the everyday operation of the army: soldiers, livestock, food, equipment, money, mail, and if required, reinforcements.

At the beginning of the Second Punic War, the Scipio brothers encountered severe logistical problems during their military campaign in Hispania. In 215, G. Scipio wrote to the Senate that he required money, clothing and wheat. He added that if they did not send him money, he would have to get it one way or another from the local people: as for the other items (clothing and wheat), there was no choice but to send them from Rome. It is apparent that G. Scipio prefered to operate in an organized manner, using his own lines of supply rather than being dependent on external elements, which were at times uncertain. The Romans in Hispania did use local produce to a certain extent and Cato declared that his army would take care of its own food, although most of the supply continued to come through the usual channels.

Scipio knew that it was practically possible to feed the army on the local produce, but there were other considerations. The main aim was to maintain good relations with the local people wherever possible. He did not wish to add more enemies to those he already had (the Carthaginians and their allies). Several years later, Scipio Aemilianus dealt with the issue of supplies through frantic preliminary preparations in Rome, early in the planning stage of the military campaign. Scipio had employed people on a voluntary basis, with no intervention from the State. Many communities in the Apennine Peninsula had donated soldiers and seafarers, equipment, weapons and food to his war against the Carthaginians.

The Roman aversion to collecting food in a hostile terrain is logical and understandable as it involved a great risk and a high potential for conflict. But there was often no choice but to collect food and infantry soldiers or horsemen were deployed to provide protection.

The Roman commanders-in-chief preferred, when possible, to purchase provisions from local people thus significantly reducing any danger to their soldiers. The Romans did exactly this during the Celtiberian wars in 195-194: they sent a *deni* (ten soldiers) to fortified hill-top cities to purchase supplies in accordance with the understandings of trade (there was no signed trade agreement) between the Romans and Celtiberians.[22]

In the sources, there are different Latin terms, which refer to different types of provisions search and collection by the army. The main are: *aquatio* (the search for water), *lignatio* (the search for wood), *pabulatio* (the search for hay to feed livestock) and *frumentario* (search for wheat and food for the people).

Groups of soldiers engaged in searching for supplies always provided a tempting easy target for all types of raider. The mountainous topography in most of Hispanic made it easy to ambush small groups of soldiers. This happened for example to L. Lucullus, who attacked the Vaccei tribes without the approval of the Senate. The Senate 'cut off' his lines of supply from Rome and in 153, Lucullus was forced to look for a solution to provide for his army, whose resources were almost exhausted. The Vaccei warriors had continuously attacked persons who had been sent to collect provisions for the army. Many Roman soldiers were killed during these missions, and in most cases the soldiers returned empty handed. The need to continuously search for provisions in a hostile area, considerably weakened his position.

In the year 151, during the siege of Palantia, local horsemen had terrorized any group of Roman soldiers sent to look for provisions. When his supplies were exhausted, Lucullus was forced to end the siege of the city and retreat with his soldiers to the winter camp.

During the siege of Numantia in the years 134 to 133, Scipio Aemilianus also provided his army with local produce collected by his soldiers, although he had a stable and regular supply line. Livius states that Scipio Aemilianus forced each soldier to carry enough wheat for thirty days.[23] Frontinus refers to the same issue and confirms the statement by Livius. The shortage of water had also become a severe problem for Aemilianus. According to Appianus, members of the Roman army began to suffer the effects of dehydration during the hot summer in the Hispanic Meseta, forcing soldiers to dig wells in the search for water. These provided small amounts of poor quality water. The soldiers were saved but they paid a high price: their horses had died due to the lack of water. Aemilianus also dictated the contents of a legionnaire's personal *sarcina* (backpack) and threw out items which he considered a luxury. Frontinus and Plutarchus said that he forbade the soldiers to carry private dishes, since he believed they were not useful and were quite redundant because of their weight. The *sarcina* was to carry only standard army tools.

Wood was one of the most important requirements. The Roman army had many uses for this commodity, mainly to build the camp for the legion, but also to provide heat for the soldiers during the cold nights. The woodcutters were at the greatest risk due to the long periods of time that they spent in one place. The locals, Celtiberians or Lusitanians, could easily hide in the woods and ambush them when they came to cut down trees. This occurred when Viriathus' warriors attacked a unit that P. Maximus sent in search of wood. Apart from protection against enemy attacks, the Roman camp filled the important role of serving as a frontline logistics base. The *hiberna* (winter camp) became the base for any long-term action, it also provided shelter for a small unit and up to an entire legion which had retreated, been ambushed or defeated.

The constant need to protect the supply lines constituted a central factor in the alignment of the army during wars. The commanders were forced to keep this in mind at all times regardless of the size of their unit, whether it be a regular supply line or a small group of soldiers sent to bring provisions for their unit during a military operation. In order to minimize the number of casualties, Roman soldiers tended to operate very quickly and only very close to their base.

The 'collectors' were usually accompanied by other soldiers. P. Maximus sent a number of legionnaires to defend a group of woodcutters during his war against the Celtiberians. Occasionally, the Romans took active protective measures against the enemy who would raid the patrols or supply convoys that were so vital for an army operating so far away from home. This is Roman counter-guerrilla warfare against the enemy. An example is an ambush that Scipio Nassica, a *pro-praetor* of Hispania Ulterior in the year 193, set against the Lusitanian warriors who had attacked his soldiers. He located and defeated the group of warriors as they were returning to their camp carrying items looted earlier from the Romans.

Chapter Four

Confronting an 'Unconventional' Enemy

This central chapter discusses the enemies that the Roman armies encountered in Hispania and how they confronted them. Also it will make an analysis of the leading Hispanic peoples: the fighting methods of the Celtiberians and Lusitanians. The discussion will focus on the important issues concerning the conduct of these tribes in war: leaders, classes of warriors, weapons, fighting methods and their origins, and how they influenced and were influenced by the Roman army.

There is little reference in the sources relating to these issues. However, the analysis of the archaeological findings plays an important role in the understanding of the link to the military history discussed in this chapter. The findings, discovered in the tombs of both Roman and native Hispanic warriors, are of the utmost importance since they serve as the main source of information regarding the weapons in use during the wars.

The Enemy and His Weapons

The Hispanic warriors were mocked and sneered at by the Roman and Greek sources. These sources were steeped in prejudice and used condescending imagery. Nonetheless, close scrutiny of these sources reveals pieces of information that shed new light on the topic and leads to a more accurate insight when combined with archaeological findings. Analysis of the data reveals one prominent fact, which is that the Hispanic peoples, especially the largest and strongest, fought as structured armies. These armies were well-organized and the command was clear and methodical. Also they were well-acquainted with Hellenistic warfare techniques, which they learned while serving as mercenaries in the Carthaginian and Hellenistic armies. They would implement these against the Roman armies in Hispania.

As in previous chapters, we know about the enemies of the Romans in the Iberian Peninsula, i.e. the leaders of the different tribes in Hispania, mainly from the Greek and Roman sources. Therefore, we need to 'translate' these sources using a 'cultural filter' to receive a more realistic picture of these tribes.

For example, when reading about certain events in the works of Polybius and Livius, it is possible to notice differences that stem from the cultural and ideological background expressed in their writing; it is likely that there will be differences between Polybius the Hellenistic, who lived in the time of the Lusitanian and Celtiberian wars, as opposed to Livius the Roman, who lived at the time of Augustus. Polybius attributes the Iberians with a certain degree of culture; but he still considers them to be barbarians. This is clear when he writes about Abilux, the Iberian king, and describes his behaviour as 'typical Iberian barbarian behaviour'.

Livius is more critical of the Iberian leaders than Polybius. He not only defines the Hispanic tribes as 'barbarians', but also specifies the flaws in the government institutions of these tribes, thus making them devoid of legitimacy in the eyes of the Romans. For example, in their view the tribal chiefs were not kings but only leaders, and not just leaders, but rather leaders of 'gangs of robbers'.[24] Livius calls them, at best, 'Regulus', a type of minor king of less importance, as it was common to call the barbarian kings in the west. Livius thinks that only Rome had a worthy regime, and therefore, only Rome was capable of awarding those barbarian tribes a worthy system of government.

Appianus, who is a much later source than Polybius and Livius (the second century AD), continues to convey the same prejudices, but he does not spare the Romans from criticism either. In an article written by Gomez Espelosin about Appianus' image of the barbarians, he writes that Appianus' slightly more balanced image of the barbarians originates from his personal status as a Greek living in the Roman world. However, he admires the power of the Roman Empire which is at its peak at the time, but he is frustrated by the barriers he is faced with as a citizen of Greek origin.

The sources all agree on one point: these leaders, the Hispanic chieftains, were also commanders-in-chief; the military leaders of the tribal armies. They also led their forces into battle against the Romans and against their intention to dominate Hispania.

The armies of the Hispanic peoples were based on infantry which constituted the major part in the military alignment of the Celtiberians and Lusitanians. The findings in archaeological excavations enable us to obtain a certain sense of the ratio between the infantry soldiers and horsemen. From findings discovered in tombs that are attributed to the Lusitanian and Vettones tribes, one of the major Celtiberian tribes, it is apparent that the number of infantry soldiers was five times more than the number of horsemen.

The sources differentiate between two types of Iberian infantry soldier, based on the type of equipment they used. The first type is the *scutati* ('heavy' infantry soldier). The other is the *caetrati* ('light' soldier). The *scutati* used a *scutum*, the large Celtic-type semi-cylindrical shield. It is quite possible that this shield arrived in the south and east of Iberia during the third century, and it is also possible that it was brought in by Hispanic mercenaries who had fought in the past as part of the Carthaginian armies. The Carthaginians probably encountered this type of shield for the first time in the wars against the Greek armies. And it is possible that the Greeks encountered and adopted this shield during their battles against the Balkan Celts.

The *caetrati* carried a *caetra*, a small rounded shield. Strabo refers to the *caetra* as a typical Lusitanian weapon. The shield was 60cm in diameter at the most, and sometimes as small as 30cm.

The *caetra* was made from strips of wood reinforced with metal strips, mainly iron. The shield was held in the left hand, and since it was relatively small, it was strong and easy to manoeuver. It was also used as a secondary offensive weapon in addition to the sword and could be used to strike the enemy's head or arms, while attacking with the sword held in the right hand. The Lusitanians were famous for being exceptionally skilled users of the *caetra*.

The combination of the *caetra* and a *falcata* (curved sword) was mostly used by Celtiberian and Lusitanian warriors.

These soldiers also wore helmets of different types, mostly made of leather and some of metal, though it is not known whether the helmets were a standard part of their attire.

The arms of the Celtiberians were not standard either; the armour was made from different materials: linen, animal fat, reinforced leather or metal sheets. These warriors sometimes wore rounded breastplates made up of metal plates attached to leather strips. These metal plates were decorated with geometric or animal symbols.

The helmets were made of leather, but from the end of the third century, the Celtiberians probably began using the Montefortino-type bronze helmet which orginated from Italy. These helmets appear on pottery decorations. Items were also discovered in excavations of Celtiberian tombs from the first and second centuries.

Le Bohec and Quesada think that these helmets arrived in Hispania with the Hispanic mercenaries who had served in the Carthaginian armies, but not directly from the Romans.

The Hispanic warriors primarily used the spear for throwing; it was some 2m long, made of iron and had a very sharp point. The Roman name for the different Celtiberian spears was *soliferrum*.[25]

The Celtiberians had a very developed metal industry, which is evident in the wide variety of weapons described in the sources, and discovered in archaeological excavations. The sources say that the weapons were of great importance in Celtiberian culture. It was an utter disgrace for a warrior to surrender or lose his weapons. It was considered as if the warrior had lost his soul, his inner being.

Celtiberian warriors from the different tribes had used different types of spears and bayonets. Heavy spearheads longer than 60cm have been discovered, and it is possible that these spears had belonged to soldiers in the heavy infantry. More common were the smaller spears, which were between 20 and 30cm long.

It is possible that the warrior who carried this type of spear carried more than one. Celtiberian and Lusitanian warriors used the spear as an 'artillery' weapon. They would cast the spears at the beginning of the battle simultaneously, with the point set on fire, in order to break up a Roman battle formation.

In addition to the spears, the Hispanic warriors also used a local version of the *pilum* and over the years, in the course of the second century, they adopted the Roman *pilum*.

Indeed, numbers of these were discovered during archaeological excavations in Spain and Portugal, in levels which is dated to the period of the Republic; but not on a site that can be unequivocally identified as to its origin. In a tomb excavation, for example, it cannot be established with any certainty who the owners of the weapons found were. The reason for that is that the Romans and the 'local' tribes, who fought against them, had sometimes used the same weapons. Only additional findings discovered in the same location can sometimes help to precisely identify and date the spears with some certainty.

It is unclear when the Hispanic peoples began using the *pilum*. In Gerona, a *pilum* that precedes the Numantine *pilum* was discovered in a layer dated to the third century.

The Republican type found in Hispania indicates that they had been in use throughout the period of the Roman conquest: from the Second Punic War in the third century up to Caesar's wars in the first century.

In Valencia, a *pilum* was discovered together with skeletons. This unique finding was interpreted by the site diggers as evidence of executions. The largest selection of *pila* was discovered in excavations in Numantia (Caseres el Viejo) and Osuna.

In some instances, unused weapons were discovered in tombs. The common explanation for this is that the Celtiberians believed in life after death. Therefore, the relationship between the warrior and his weapon would continue after death. Celtiberian warriors were buried with new weapons.

Excavations in Teruel have uncovered both light and heavy *pila*. These two groups are dated to the first half of the first century BC. The spears were discovered alongside local helmets, swords and the remains of a catapult probably used in the wars of Sertorius.

The most recognizable sword to be identified with the Hispanic peoples is the *Gladius Hispaniensis* ('Spanish sword'): a short weapon some 60 to 65cm in length, which was the typical Celtiberian weapon. Over the years, the sword underwent several alterations when it was 'adopted' by the Roman army as the main personal weapon of the infantry soldiers.

The Hispanic peoples used two types, a straight and a curved type of *gladius*. The straight type was typically used by the Celtiberians, and the curved type was used by the Iberians of the Mediterranean coastal regions.

Both types were adopted by Roman soldiers, but only the straight sword had survived the period of the Republic and had become the main weapon by the end of the Republic and the period of the *Principate*.

Quesada, who studied the relation between the Iberian weapons and Roman fighting techniques in general, in particular the development of the 'Hispanic *gladius*' until it became the standard weapon for the Roman army, claims that it is a local version, which evolved from the ancient Gaelic *gladius* of the La Tenne 1 type. Connolly, who studied nine collections of weapons from the Republic's time in Gaul, the Balkans and Hispania, also supports Quesada's view. This view is now accepted as correct and adopted by most of those researching the weapon.

The Romans probably first encountered the *gladius* in Hispania and many have been discovered in Cerro de las Balas (Seville) and Graccurris (Alfaro, Rioja). In both cases, these were clearly dated to the second century BC. When Julius Caesar fought in Gaul in the first century, the Roman version of the *gladius* had already become standard equipment in the Roman army, whereas the Gauls had already replaced the long sword with a longer version.

Diodorus says that these swords were so strong that neither helmet nor shield provided protection.

Seneca cites the story of a legionnaire who fought under the command of Julius Caesar in Hispania, in the first century during the civil wars. In the battle of Munda, the legionnaire suffered a severe head wound when his helmet was destroyed beyond recognition. He lost an eye and his cranial bone was broken due to a blow from a 'Spanish sword'.

It is most likely that this story was a figment of Seneca's imagination or that of his source, yet it illustrates the reputation that the 'Spanish sword' had even in Seneca's time in the first century AD.

The Hispanic peoples also had cavalry. In fact, in most battles the Celtiberian cavalry had a numerical advantage over their Roman counterparts. Horses were held in high regard in the rituals and art of the Hispanic peoples. In several excavations, numerous figurines have been discovered, some made of copper but most are of clay, in the shape of a horse or of mounted cavalrymen.

Horses and cavalrymen were also common themes on ceramics made by the Hispanic peoples. Strabo praises the beauty and strength of the Iberian horse and compares them to horses from the Euphrates area. Strabo also mentions that occasionally, two cavalrymen would share a horse and ride for long distances. The Hispanic horsemen were very active in the wars against the Romans and also in warfare between the tribes. Although the Hispanic peoples used horsemen in the fourth century, it was probably the Carthaginians who had developed the Iberian cavalry, when they organized their army by copying that of foreign mercenaries. Iberian horsemen were seen and were active not only in Hispania; in the Hellenistic world, the Hispanic horsemen served as mercenaries in the different armies.

The Celtiberian horsemen filled a wide variety of tasks in their military alignment. These tasks included gathering intelligence about the enemy movements in general, and specific intelligence before a battle, misleading the enemy in battle, and to a lesser extent, a frontal assault on the Roman cavalry. The weapons carried by the Celtiberian cavalry were probably similar to those used by the infantry.

Horsemen were not the only Hispanic 'export' to the Carthaginian and Hellenistic worlds. The Carthaginian infantry contained numbers of soldiers from the Iberian Peninsula, and these warriors, especially the Celtiberian and Lusitanians, were in high demand as mercenaries throughout the Hellenistic world. The reason for this was probably their military prowess, however their motivation to join the army was a shortage of land and poverty in the peninsula. Iberian warriors are mentioned as early as the year 480, in the Sicily Wars, where they fought, first as mercenaries for the Carthaginians and then for the Sicilian Greeks. Between 409 and 408, Hispanic forces took part in the conquest of Selinunte and Himera; in the year 406 they fought in Agrigentum; in the years 405 to 404 they were involved in the siege of Syracuse, which ended the Second Punic-Greek War (409 to 404). In the years 397 to 395, they fought once again in the Third Punic-Greek War during another siege of Syracuse. Livius writes that Hispanic mercenaries obeyed the commands of their own commanders and that they lived in separate camps. Also, they held internal councils and decided whether and where to fight.

These mercenaries sometimes chose to fight against other Celtiberians who served in the armies that were the rivals of their employers. References to Hispanic mercenaries fighting with the Greek armies can also be found in the works of Thucydides and Plutarchus. Celtiberians did fight with regular and organized armies, but it seems that this did not have an impact on their combat methods in their homeland against the Romans.

In addition, there is no evidence from sources or archaeological excavations that the Hispanic peoples besieged cities or built war machines.

Based on the course of the battles against the Romans and their outcome, it is very likely that despite the fact that the Celtiberians did not adopt the Hellenistic fighting methods, they did study their manoeuvering in battle and that did helped them considerably when fighting the Roman military. The Hispanic peoples were aware of the events around the Mediterranean; Hellenistic culture did have an influence, more so in coastal areas than inland but less so in the northwest of the Iberian Peninsula.

This is the background for understanding the fighting methods that the Hispanic peoples employed against the Roman armies, and clearly proves certain knowledge of Roman fighting methods that were also based on Hellenistic methods. The Hispanic soldiers should not be seen as wild warriors who lived at the end of the world disconnected from the 'big Mediterranean world', who encountered for the first time an enemy that fought 'conventionally', but rather as experienced warriors who were familiar with the different fighting methods. We will see this clearly in the next subsection on the analysis of the largest revolt that had taken place in Hispania against the Romans – the Lusitanian revolt led by Viriathus.

Limitations of exercising power – the failure of the army intelligence

High-quality intelligence is of great importance for any military success. Gathering intelligence has always been a task of the utmost importance to any army, both in ancient times and today. The Romans knew this fact but never developed an independent intelligence corps, in the modern sense of the word. The Senate in Rome did not receive information concerning events in Hispania from independent and organized sources, and had to rely on information passed on by the commanders in the field. As a result, the Senate's control of the army operating in Hispania was quite, if not very, weak. The personal capabilities of each individual military commander determined the quality of tactical intelligence. As we will see later on, this was manifested numerous times during the Hispanic wars where the local tribes ambushed Roman forces.

The Romans used *exploratores* (scouts) to gather tactical intelligence. These were neither fixed nor designated groups, but infantry soldiers and mostly horsemen who were used for specific missions. Although the *exploratores* were used for many missions, the most important source of intelligence for Romans army commanders in Hispania was the local population: leaders of tribes, paid collaborators, ordinary people and prisoners of war. The Roman army did have some success with intelligence gathering, but it also had many failures.

The structure of the Roman army at the time of the Republic, the command chain in particular, was not compatible to the creation of a permanent and dedicated intelligence section.

Senior position holders, both in the cities and provinces, were replaced each year and even holders of special roles (*pro-magistrates*) served no more than two or three years. The Senate at times of military campaigns was almost completely dependent on receiving reports from provincal governors or a commander in the field. An excellent example is the conduct of Julius Caesar during his war in Gaul, when he made sure that the Roman Senate and populace would receive only the information that was of benefit to himself. The Senate, having no alternate sources of intelligence, was forced to take Caesar's reports at face value.

While serving as a governor in Cilicia, Cicero criticized the fact that there was no central body that would provide intelligence services to the governors of 'problematic' provinces, who were in need of such information. In practice, this meant that when the commanders of the army set out to war they were venturing into the unknown and dependent on their own abilities. Julius Caesar succeeded in doing so in Gaul, yet Crassus failed in his war against the Parthian kingdom, where his army was destroyed.

In my opinion, the best example of a good personal ability that used high-quality intelligence to achieve a magnificent victory is that of Publius Cornelius Scipio at Nova Cartago. The works of Polybius describe his exact planning of every step of the operation. Scipio examined the relationship between the local population and the Carthaginians living in the city, also the relationship between the different Carthaginian factions, as well as information regarding the size and quality of the forces defending city.

In addition, he inspected the location of the city which helped him determine his direction of attack and a line of retreat in the case of a defeat.

Polybius does not provide information regarding the ways in which Scipio Africanus obtained the information, apart from that concerning the lagoon surrounding the city which was received from local fishermen.

Scipio firstly assessed the three Carthaginian armies that operated in the area, and then decided which to attack first. Following a careful evaluation of the situation in the field, he noted that Nova Cartago was the focal point for the Carthaginian government in Hispania; the city served as the administrative, logistic, industrial and military centre for the Carthaginians in the Iberian Peninsula. Conquest of this city could eliminate the need for numerous battles – and the possibility of defeat – and strike a decisive blow against the Carthaginian presence in Hispania. The conquest of the city led to a swift victory. This was not the first time that Scipio Africanus displayed an impressive ability to use obtained information. Frontinus notes that when a delegation led by Laelius was sent to King Siphax, Scipio sent with him tribunes and centurions disguised as slaves to spy in his camp; their mission was to gather intelligence on the number and quality of their troops and the layout of the camp. To achieve this, the spies released a horse then chased it all over the camp, all the time gathering information about the defences. This act was essential then, as it is now, in order to prepare a plan of battle. In most cases, the Roman armies operating in Hispania during the second century were relatively small and operated over large areas, usually unknown to them.

Sometimes it was difficult for the Romans to even locate the enemy. But their enemy – who would be well acquainted with their own terrain – had a much better chance of locating the Romans advancing deep into his territory and remain undetected until the moment of his attack.

The horsemen, in the main an auxiliary force of non-Roman soldiers, collected most of the intelligence except that from the mountain areas where the *exploratores* were deployed. These small units worked ahead of the main army. A Roman commander on receiving this information would be aware of the enemy's location and military strength allowing the preparation of an effective battle plan. Livius, in his book which deals with the battles of the fourth century mentions the use of scouts several times and also in his book on the war against Hannibal. For example, in the year 314, Roman magistrates sent scouts to check whether a rumour regarding a Gallic invasion was true and to observe the actions of the Gauls. In 304, scouts were used to discover the battle plans of the Aequi tribe. Livius also tells that Fabius Maximus deployed scouts to track the movements of Hannibal in Italy.

In all these cases, it was not a dedicated 'patrol force', but as Ezov has proven in his research on the 'Roman scouts' was a group of warriors selected by a commander for the execution of a specific intelligence-gathering mission. It was crucial for these scouts to operate hidden from the enemy, but it was essential to locate the enemy and gather vital information as to the strength of his forces, before the commander planned his next moves.

The Romans also deployed *speculatores* (spies) as the secret arm of the field intelligence. Fewer in number than the scouts, they carried the responsibility of operating covertly in enemy territory. The sources describe several instances in which spies were used in Hispania to gather tactical intelligence, from the period of the Scipio brothers at the end of the third century to the revolt by Sertorius.

Higher echelon commanders had not always operated according to the rules specified above, which sometimes resulted in entire armies being destroyed. This was the case in the year 152, when C. Vitalius pursued the Lusitanian warriors of Viriathus deep into their territory. He had ignored the rules of safety as he entered into unknown terrain without any intelligence regarding the enemy forces and fell into a deadly trap; he entered a narrow valley between wooded hills with his entire army. The Lusitanians were waiting in ambush and attacked from the front and sides; Vitalius and 6,000 of his men were killed.

The amount and quality of intelligence that was available to a Roman commander in the field also depended on his own knowledge of the territory in which he operated. If it was an area in which the Roman army had previously operated, such as south and east Hispania, the commander would have had reasonable quality information, although not necessarily up-to-date. Therefore, it was safer to avoid, as much as possible, venturing too far away from familiar territory. This is how Fabius Maximus always operated by moving his forces along the coast; an area that the Romans knew very well and thought to be relatively safe. He preferred not to take any chances by entering inland areas under the control of Viriathus.

Gathering geographic information about an area in which an attack was about to be launched for the first time, was also of vital importance. Roman commanders operated in various ways to obtain this information, but there is little detail in the sources. It is possible that the writers did not consider this subject to be important and since most of them had no military knowledge it is very likely they were totally unfamiliar with this subject. Writers such as Polybius and Julius Caesar, who were military men, did make brief reference to the subject.

A geographic survey that Scipio Aemilianus ordered Polybius to carry out before the invasion to North Africa in the Third Punic War, serves as an excellent illustration of its importance. Pliny the Elder wrote that Aemilianus sent Polybius by ship to the coast of North Africa in order to map the area. Julius Caesar provides another example; he worked very hard to gather geographic and ethnographic information about Britain while preparing for his invasion. When he realized that the information received from traders, from Gallic tribes and others, was insufficient and very unreliable, he sent Gnaius Velusianus and ordered him to bring any type of information that he could gather. In cases when the Roman army was supposed to operate in unknown regions, such as Lusitania or Cantabria, the intelligence was, at best, sparse and inadequate.

High-quality intelligence has always been crucial for the success of a military campaign. In the case of a war against an enemy that uses guerrilla warfare, the importance is multiplied.

In the year 137, C. Hostilius Mancius and his entire army were ambushed by Celtiberian soldiers after entering into unreconnoitred unknown territory with only minimal information regarding enemy forces. Eventually, Mancius was forced to surrender in order to save his men from death or captivity.

It was possible to defeat an elusive enemy which used guerrilla tactics if their base was located. Also if the attack was timed for when the leader was present it would strike a decisive blow on the enemy and save many lives. In order to succeed on such a mission, careful reconnaissance of the terrain and the location of the enemy is vital. Therefore, the local population served as an important source of intelligence gathering, especially the leaders of the different tribes. Asturian 'traitors' provided information to the Roman army about the movements of the Asturian army, which had planned to ambush the army of Augustus as it marched, in regulation three lines, through narrow valleys and gorges between the mountains.

Those allies who lived outside the Roman-controlled area also provided an important source of intelligence. An event detailed by Frontinus shows how Roman policy – documented in the sources, the Romans took prisoners in order to force a ceasefire, or to serve as a ransom, or as a sign of loyalty to Rome – was also used to establish friendly relations on the basis of an exchange of interests. Frontinus states that Scipio Africanus returned a girl to a family of the local nobility who had been captured during the campaign to conquest Nova Cartago. Not only did he return her, but also when he found out that she was getting married, he returned her with gold charms similar to those her parents had used to pay for her release. When the tribe heared of his deed, the entire tribe was overawed by his act, and decided to change to the Roman side as the war continued.[26]

It is very likely that prisoners of war were also used as a source of intelligence, whether with their consent or not. The Romans had other 'passive' ways of obtaining tactical intelligence, including initiatives for receiving intelligence from other sources, voluntary or compulsory. One of these ways was through the client states or clients. The Greek city of Massilia for example, played a very important role in the Second Punic War when its citizens informed the Romans that Hannibal had crossed the Pyrenees and was mobilizing many forces in Gaul. Two ships from Massilia served C. Scipio as a 'maritime patrol force' collecting intelligence of the Carthaginian maritime movements south of the river Ebro.

Deserters and refugees also served as sources of intelligence. In the case of deserters, the information was provided voluntarily out of the wish to gain legitimacy in the eyes of their captors. Local citizens usually collaborated with occupying forces, hoping that it would leave their settlement as soon as possible. Vegetius had written that the locals served as an important source of information, especially when they served as guides. However, he adds that it was important to crosscheck any information received with other sources.

Prisoners of war and other prisoners also served as sources of intelligence, although there had been many limitations. First, we should keep in mind that the information was obtained from them by force and therefore not always reliable. Secondly, most of the prisoners of war were simple warriors and the information they possessed was limited, like one stone of a complete mosaic that the captor needs to assemble in order to see the big picture.

It should be mentioned that the Romans conducted extensive diplomatic activities in their travels across the empire; an intelligence-gathering activity of great importance. Roman representatives, usually army officers, made contact with friendly tribe leaders. These agreed, for different reasons, to provide the Romans with information concerning rival tribes, usually their neighbours, though they preferred not to do this directly. The information received from the chieftains was not always reliable or truthful which made it impossible to trust the help received from them or their tribes; some tribes were not politically stable and a number were dependent on the prestige and power of the chieftain and his ability to unite the entire tribe. Yet when it came to the Roman ability to obtain information in a foreign territory, there was no substitute for a friendly relationship with the tribes. That was at least until they were able to capture prisoners who could provide up-to-date, firsthand information on the status of their forces.

There is little information about the different ploys used by the Roman army to gather required information. As there also is on how this information was managed, how it was stored, and how it was used.

Who was the person at the army headquarters responsible for managing the gathered information? Was there a person in charge of processing or decoding the intelligence, or was this part of the role of the commander in the field? Existing sources take the trouble to specify that intelligence collection was one of the most important characteristics of every commander in the army. But in practice those who were engaged in this task, such as Scipio Aemilianus and Julius Caesar, indicate that Roman army commanders did not have an organized and fixed method for intelligence gathering; as stated before, it was dependent upon the personal ability of the supreme commander in the field to obtain the information and process it in the correct way.

Enemy's Warfare Tactics: Guerrilla Warfare

The guerrilla-warfare tactics used against the Romans in Hispania did not receive much attention in ancient sources. The writers were not interested in this type of warfare and most were not familiar with military tactics.

They described several 'unusual' methods and 'inappropriate' tactics used by the leaders of numerous 'bands of robbers'. But analysis of the sources reveals a completely different picture: different combat methods were employed by organized armies with an organized chain of command based on a well-planned fighting strategy. These combat methods had been inserted into the consciousness of the Lusitanian youths during their 'rites of passage' to adulthood.

The Romans misunderstood and misinterpreted the 'unconventional' methods used by the young local warriors. As we see later on, due to this misinterpretation the Romans missed many chances of victory, or became the victims of a crushing defeat.

The political situation in Hispania where there was no coordination between the many tribes, resulting in a lack of 'pan-Hispanic patriotism', greatly helped the Romans through the many wars. Even Viriathus, the celebrated leader of the great Lusitanian revolt (who will be the focus in this subsection) did not succeed in unifying the Hispanic peoples. They preferred not to break their treaty with Rome.

The type of guerrilla warfare tactics that the Hispanic tribes used against the Romans, as well as each other, was considered as a perfectly natural and accepted way to fight. Diodorus tells us that when Lusitanian youths came of age, they armed themselves with weapons and went into the the hills, there they formed into large groups and ventured out on so-called military campaigns to accumulate booty by raiding other tribes. It is interesting to note that Diodorus speaks of these raids as traditional customs and not as a result of a definitive need. Van Gennep defined this as a *'rites de passage'*, a demonstration of physical and mental strength to the society of the adult warriors. The Romans did not consider this type of activity as a matter of honour, tradition or culture, but called them sweepingly *latrolistes* ('gangs') and their leaders were called *latrorum dux* ('gang leaders').

Strabo wrote that the Celtiberians were incapable of establishing large confederations, and that they wasted their resources on inter-tribal conflicts. However, it is know that the Celtiberians could often form an army of thousands of warriors, and therefore it seems that Strabo's account is inaccurate. It is likely that Strabo's report is merely an outcome of prejudice, and nothing else. It seems that the Celtiberian problem did not lie in forming an army, but in the correct exploitation of it following the battle, i.e. how to take full advantage of the victory. Appianus provided a different, social-economic angle to this issue; he thinks that the Celtiberians had to resort to a life of gangs and highway robbers due to poverty, which he thinks was caused by a lack of lands.

Based on their combat doctrine, Celtiberian warriors would make a frontal attack and in no particular formation – this is at least how it was seen by the Romans. The warriors would suddenly halt their attack and retreat from the battlefield. This is why the Romans had the impression that they were running away. This process of attack and retreat was repeated over and over again.

The Romans would repeatedly pursue them in an organized battle formation according to Roman fighting rules. The intention of the Celtiberians was to taunt the Romans into forgetting their discipline and set out on an unrestrained pursuit. They would then suddenly halt their retreat, reorganize and launch a deadly counterattack. According to Appianus, the Roman legion was less manoeuvrable than the Celtiberian enemy, as the heavily-equipped Roman legionnaires could not move easily in a one-on-one battle and therefore had a slim chance of surviving this type of attack.

The Romans viewed this type of fighting as a lack of tactics and battle planning, and even as an irrational and cowardly conduct. Livius wrote that the Celtiberians panicked and often sought a place of refuge. It seems that Livius, who was not a military man, failed to understand Celtiberian and Lusitanian tactics. The reality was, in fact, far different to Livius' view: actually, the implementation of the tactic of retreat, regroup and counterattack with a relatively large force required a very high level of command and planning.

There is evidence that the Romans also employed this method. Appianus wrote that S. Gracchus had retreated after a hard battle and let the Celtiberians enter his camp, full of confidence of their triumph. When the Celtiberians lost control and began plundering the camp, Gracchus suddenly returned and attacked and defeated them.

The Lusitanians' main objective was to break the Roman formation and divide the battle into units fighting one-on-one, as they had little or no chance of winning an 'organized' battle. In one-on-one battles, the Romans lost all their tactical advantage which allowed the Celtiberians, who often had the advantage of large numbers, to indulge in their preferred method of fighting.

The Iberian peoples occasionally deployed the infantry together with their cavalry.

In the year 195, the Roman cavalry found it very difficult to break through the rows of the Turdethanians. Livius says that a combined attack by both Turdethanian infantry and cavalry had almost forced the Roman to break their battle formation. The pro-consul P. Marcellus ordered his cavalry to attack, and only then did the Romans managed to overcome the enemy, although with great difficulty.

The Lusitanian war in general, and the war to crush the revolt by Viriathus in particular, are the most prominent examples of the clash between two totally different schools of combat: the classic school of the Roman army and the 'unconventional' school of the Hispanic tribes in general and the Lusitanians in particular.

In a period of over twenty years, between 154 and 133, the Romans had been engaged in two of the most severe wars they had ever known in Hispania: the Lusitanian war and the Numantine war (also known as the Celtiberian war). These two wars, especially the Lusitanian, were characterized by intensive guerrilla warfare against the Romans. These wars began with the refusal by the Celtiberian city of Segeda to take down its walls and ended with its fall and the destruction of Numantia.

Appianus is the most important source of information on the Lusitanian war, and especially Viriathus. The common view in research is that Appianus' main source was Polybius. It is very likely that Appianus arrived at Polybius through sources that were later, but preceded Appainus: Livius, Diodorus Siculus, Plutarchus, and Poseidonius (which is fragmented and arrived at through other sources) and others whose names are unknown.

Despite the stated sources of Appianus, we should keep in mind, as Astin writes, his sources are not certain and these are all scholarly speculations.

Appianus describes the Lusitanian war in relatively great detail, but he has done so while simultaneously describing the Celtiberian war, which took place at the same time in another region of Hispania: he basically 'skips' in his writings between the two wars, which makes the text hard to read.

The second most important source of information on the wars of Viriathus is Diodorus Siculus, who wrote of Viriathus in his 23rd book, only a small part of which has survived. There are differences between the two sources, which probably indicate that they used different sources. It is possible that Poseidonius was the main source for Diodorus, and not Polybius.

According to Appianus, the Lusitanian war began when the Lusitanians, led by Punicus, raided the areas controlled by the Romans. They defeated the *praetors* Manillius and Piso, then joined forces with the Vettones and advanced to the Mediterranean coast, and even to North Africa. The *praetors* Mummius followed by Atilius, succeeded in halting and pushing the Lusitanians back to their country after years of battles and intermittent periods of peace. These events were previously reviewed in this work, and therefore I will move directly to Viriathus and his revolt against the Romans.

Viriathus, the leader of the Lusitanian revolt, is described in the Greek and Roman sources from different points of view. Each one of the sources has taken a position corresponding to his interest, and evidently Viriathus is always regarded as the enemy of the Roman Republic, which was the main subject of the Greek and Roman sources.

Diodorus Siculus, Appianus and Dio Cassius not only refer to the military aspects and leadership qualities of Viriathus (all three agree on his qualities as a warrior and leader), but also to his character, although not in great detail.

These three sources lay the foundation to Virithus' image, as it is known in research (as well as in Spanish and Portuguese folklore). The folklore, which is based on these sources, presents Viriathus as a shepherd who grew up in the area of Mons Herminius, present-day northern Portugal.

Diodorus, the only writer who had referred to the issue of place of birth, wrote that Viriathus came from the Lusitanian tribes that lived on the coast. However, Diodorus did not mention which sea. Alarcão, who studied the familiarity of the ancient sources within Hispanic geography, wondered whether Diodorus referred to the river Ebro; the Celtiberian tribes lived to the south, and the Lusitanians to the north.

However, as we see later on, Viriathus' knowledge of the topography of the battleground and the different fighting methods he demonstrated, attest that he was not necessarily a shepherd and that he did not come from the north, but probably from south or central Portugal. In later Roman sources, Viriathus had already gained the reputation of a national hero or freedom fighter. These sources mentioned above, tell of a typical individual from the Hispanic peoples, a man who wins the admiration of his *devotii* (followers) who are prepared to die for their leader. Appianus even describes the funeral procession for Viriathus, after 200 interim battles had taken place between Lusitanian warriors in honour of their murdered leader. Ammianus Marcellinus wrote at the end of fourth century AD, some 500 years after the Lusitanian war, and compared Viriathus to Spartacus.

The Lusitanian War resumed in the year 151, when S. Galba, the new *praetor* of Hispania Ulterior, set out on a journey towards Lusitania at the head of an army of 15,000 soldiers. He marched his army straight into a 'honey trap' set by the Lusitanians, who had employed their favoured method of attack and retreat. Not realizing that this was the Lusitanian battle plan, Galba began pursuing them through the mountains. On that fateful day some 7,000 soldiers, around half of Galba's army, were killed. Galba, with the remains of his army, fled to Carmo.

Later, Galba and L. Lucullus, the *praetor* of Hispania Citerior, decided to join forces against the Lusitanians. They tried to provoke the Lusitanians into starting a war, but they would not be tempted. Even when taking a different approach by systematically destroying villages and crops, the Romans were still unsuccessful in provoking the Lusitanians to enter into battle. Frustrated, Galba and Lucullus turned to the option of deceit and betrayal and eventually massacred the Lusitanians. These actions have already been described previously, and their outcome was the largest ever revolt against the Romans in Hispania. Some of the army camps that the Romans built around Lusitania in order to crush the revolt, were discovered in archaeological excavations in the last decades. Basically, they constitute the majority of the Roman army camps from the time of the Republic to be discovered in the Iberian Peninsula.

In the year 147, some 10,000 Lusitanians attacked an area under Roman control and advanced to Osuna, where they were surrounded by the army of C. Vetilius. The less than tactful Vetilius offered to them exactly what Lucullus and Galba had offered several years earlier: land in exchange for their weapons.

Viriathus, who was one of the Lusitanian warriors, as well as one of the survivors of the Galba massacre, managed to incite the Lusitanian army against his leader and take his place. The memory of that massacre was still fresh in the mind of Viriathus, and he refused to surrender to the Romans. He chose 1,000 horsemen and carried out a diversionary attack against the Romans. By doing this he helped most of his army to escape from the Roman siege. Viriathus also carried out several lightning attacks and retreats in order to delay the Romans, while his Lusitanian infantry soldiers fled in different directions according to precise planning. Vetilius who was furious, chased the Lusitanians into the heart of their country and in his haste fell into a trap. He entered a gorge between wooded hills with an army of 10,000 infantry and and 300 horsemen, where the legionnaires found it difficult to manoeuvre in such confined terrain due to their heavy equipment. Although a veteran officer Vetilius entered the gorge with his 'eyes wide open'; he probably thought that a victory was achievable due to his numerical advantage. The Lusitanians attacked from an ambush position and Vetilius and 6,000 of his soldiers were killed. Diodorus recounts that Vetilius had been killed by a Lusitanian warrior who did not recognize him thinking that he was an ordinary, fat and old soldier.

Viriathus twice defeated C. Plautius, the next *praetor*. The first was when he destroyed a force of 4,000 Roman soldiers. The second was when he defeated a force which had pursued the Lusitanians into their territory near Mons Veneris.

Following this victory, Viriathus worked hard on gaining the support of as many Celtiberian tribes as possible. He was actually attempting to win the role an all-Iberian leader fighting against the Roman conqueror, when in fact even the Lusitanians were not united. Viriathus did so by telling stories of his personal bravery, while inflating the ratio of his disadvantage in his battles against the Romans, and shattering the myth of the Romans being invincible. At the same he terrorized the many tribes who had remained loyal to the Romans. According to the sources, Viriathus obliterated Segobriga one of the major Celtiberian cities.

It is noteworthy that in excavations carried out to date in Cabeza del Griego, a site which is identified as Segobriga, the archaeologists have not uncovered any findings dated prior to the first century BC. If the identification of the site as Segobriga is correct, then it is possible that this event is no more than a product of local folklore, which was formed over time on the tradition that was created about Viriathus.

That year, the Romans had conquered the city of Carthage, which led to the ending of the Third Punic War. Now, the Romans could direct considerable resources to the war in Hispania.

In the year 145, the Senate appointed Q. Fabius Maximus, the conqueror of Greece and adopted son of Aemilius Paulus, as the governor of Hispania Ulterior. Maximus preferred to recruit new soldiers instead of taking the veterans who had just returned from the wars in Greece.

The Senate appointed C. Laelius as the governor of Hispania Citerior. The two governors now had forces totalling 15,000 new legionnaires, 2,000 horsemen and ten elephants. F. Maximus spent a year training his forces in the area of Baetica, ignoring repeated attempts by Viriathus to lure him into battle before he was ready.

A year later, when Maximus felt that his army was ready to fight he launched an attack. He always attempted to move his army along the coast and not risk moving inland, an area mostly under the control of Viriathus. However, he did have to send groups of soldiers into the forests to collect wood and these were repeatedly attacked. The Lusitanians also repeatedly, especially in the area of Gades, ambushed his forces and inflicted heavy losses

Fabius had won the first battle, in a frontal attack on Viriathus who retreated to Cordoba after suffering heavy losses. This was the first triumph that the Romans had achieved in battle in Hispania for the past nineteen years.

Viriathus, who was probably aware of his limitations, especially in terms of troop numbers, signed treaties with several established Celtiberian tribes: the Arevacii, Belli and Titii. This is how he had become the primary cause of the additional Celtiberian revolt. Viriathus had hoped that the Romans would not have enough soldiers to fight on two fronts simultaneously.

In the years 143 to 142, Viriathus was successful in retaking territories lost in the previous year, and he even gained military superiority in the region of Baetica, south Hispania. C. Pompeius, the new governor of Hispania Citerior, suffered heavy losses in his failed attempt to stop Viriathus.

Rome learned of the deteriorating situation in Hispania through reports, rumours and information from soldiers who had returned home after completing their military service. In order to prevent a total collapse of the forces, the consul Q. Fabius Maximus Servilianus was sent to Hispania at the head of a large consular army – in terms of Hispania – two legions totalling 18,000 infantry and 1,600 horsemen.

In addition, Servilianus received auxiliary soldiers and ten elephants from Numidia.

After several battles mostly won by the Romans, although not conclusively, Viriathus went back to employing the tactic in which he excelled: attack and retreat.

In a battle near Itucca, the Romans lost 3,000 soldiers, and it appeared that the enemy had been defeated. They set off in pursuit of their enemy, who had 'fled in panic', but then the Lusitanians halted and carried out a swift and deadly counterattack. The Lusitanians pursued the Romans up to their camp, where the rout almost turned into a massacre.

Servilianus barely managed to repel the attack and hold out until night. When darkness came the Lusitanians, who would not fight at night due to religious beliefs, left the battlefield.[27]

Despite his many successes, Viriathus was forced to retreat to Lusitania, as his army had become battle-weary. He probably had not succeeded in recruiting sufficient numbers from the Baetica tribes, and his lines of supply had become too long and unstable.

Servilianus quickly managed to take advantage of Viriathus' vulnerability, and re-conquered most of the territories previously lost in the war, especially in the valley between the river Guadalquivir and the river Guadiana and along the coastal strip in the south-central Hispania. In this military campaign, Servilianus defeated two Lusitanian tribe leaders, whose original names are unknown to us, but are known by the Roman names detailed by Appianus: Curius and Apuleius. Appianus describes them as 'gang leaders', as he usually does, and as is customary in the classic sources.

Two problems, or severe defects, are apparent in the fighting method used by Viriathus. Firstly, he was unable to consolidate his control in the territories that he occupied after impressive victories. Secondly, despite all his impressive triumphs, the reputation of Rome among Hispanic peoples remained stable. Although Viriathus was considered a 'local hero', he did not succeed in winning over many local tribes to his side and recruit their people into his army.

At this point, it is necessary to compare the state of Viriathus to that of Hannibal in Italy after his battle in Cannae. In Italy, at that time, as well as in Hispania, the safest course of action for the local tribes was to remain loyal to Rome, and not to support the 'freedom fighter': in addition, it should be taken into account that in the Iberian Peninsula, there had been no awareness of an 'Iberian' or 'Lusitanian' nation, the same as there had been no awareness of an 'Italian' nation in the Apennine Peninsula. It is quite possible that Viriathus was aware of these defects and difficulties. The limitation of his power was also clear to him, and only this can explain his decisions following the battle near the city of Erisana.

Viriathus made a fierce attack on the Roman army besieging the city of Erisana. He out-flanked their forces and managed to drive them into a narrow gulley that ended in a cliff face. Viriathus then made a move that surprised both the Romans and Lusitanians. Instead of annihilating the Roman army he offered Servilianus a peace treaty to sign, which was favourable to Rome: respect the borders of Lusitania and recognition in its status as '*amici populi romani*' (friends of the Roman people). Most of the treaties between tribal chiefs and Roman commanders in the field were in effect a dictation of terms to the *sponsio* ('defeated party'). These were treaties that did not require further approval from higher ranks on both sides, neither the tribal council nor Rome. Presumably, the Romans regarded these treaties as a step toward total surrender by the barbarians. In addition, it is likely that these, which were in fact ceasefire treaties, were signed with 'gang leaders' defined by Appianus as not to be considered worthy of attention by the Roman Senate.

But this time it was a different treaty, an official *foedus* ('treaty') which the Romans signed between two equal parties, at least theoretically.[28] Rome only signed this type of treaty with states or independent political entities capable of organizing an independent foreign policy.

This type of treaty would provide an added value to Viriathus, as he had hoped that it would lead to Roman recognition of him as a legitimate king. Nonetheless, Appianus never related to this event in his writings. Due to the importance of this treaty, it was later approved also by the Roman Senate.

Viriathus was certainly aware of his limitations, and especially of the Roman advantages. He saw how the Romans succeeded in sending forces time and again to Hispania despite repeated defeats. It is very likely that Viriathus had feared that he would lose the war against the Romans in the long run, despite his many victories, and decided to compromise.

It is not a trivial matter to make difficult decisions during war, and carry on with the exisiting situation; this requires an overall strategic vision and strong leadership. Viriathus probably had both. In contrast, he probably did not have specialist administrative capabilities. As far as we can tell from the sources, Viriathus harboured no plans to establish any sovereign political entity in case he succeeded in getting rid of the Romans.

Either way, those in Rome were not pleased with the treaty signed between Servilianus and Viriathus, and managed to cancel it after a short time. In the year 140, the consul Q. Servilius Caepius, brother of Servilianus, and the *praetor* Popilius Laenas were sent to Hispania, their objective was to get rid of Viriathus, once and for all. Firstly, the Roman army managed to surprise Viriathus and then pursue him into the Meseta mountains on the Lusitanian border. In the year 139, Caepius attacked the Vettones and Callaicii, neighbours of the Lusitanians, to the north and east and their allies.

M. Popillius Laenas, governor of Hispania Citerior, also participated in the battles. Viriathus, who found himself surrounded by two armies attempted to negotiate with the Roman commanders. He first tried with Laenas, but when he demanded that Viriathus surrender unconditionally, he turned to Caepius. This move led to the death of Viriathus.

All the sources suggest that he was murdered, although their versions differ. The differences are not immense and the researchers tend to usually accept the version by Appianus, in which Caepius bribed the Lusitanian representatives to murder Viriathus.

However, the version by Diodorus Siculus should also be cited. His version differs in that the names of the Lusitanian representatives are different to those stated by Appianus. According to Siculus – and this is the major difference – the Lusitanian representatives offered to murder Viriathus in return for benefits from the Romans (this is how he clears Caepius of being responsible for the murder). Either way, the Romans had finally succeeded in removing Viriathus: the leader who had terrified them, and described by Dio Cassius as the best among Hispanic leaders. Appianus wrote, he was not the best in battle, but used bribery and murder.[29]

The Lusitanians continued using guerrilla-warfare tactics after the murder of Viriathus, but since there was no unifying leadership, their warriors could do nothing other than wear down the Romans.

Appianus writes that 'Lusitanian groups' who had been influenced by Viriathus, employed guerrilla tactics against Junius Brutus, who did not known how to respond to these attacks: or according to Appianus had seen no benefit in pursuing these gangs, and instead employed a scorched earth policy, and burned down crops in the fields, attacked villages and killed civilians. This was his way of deterring the Lusitanians, and ending their attacks.

Laqueur provides two reasons as to why the Hispanic peoples utilized guerrilla warfare. The first is that warriors from these peoples had served for many years as mercenaries with the Greeks, Phoenicians and Carthaginians (they were the majority in the Carthaginian army). During their military service, they had learned and perfected the method of attack and retreat combat as well as conventional fighting methods.

Laqueur's second reason is that the mountainous and forested topography of the Iberian Peninsula prepared the local peoples to use fighting methods which adapt to the terrain.

In the Cantabrian and Asturian wars, the native warriors very skillfully used their knowledge of the mountainous terrain, with its narrow, winding valleys and gorges, of North Hispania. Dio Cassius recounts that in the year 26, some 180 years after Rome had launched their campaign to conquer Hispania, the Asturians and Cantabrians attacked the armies of Augustus and Agrippa, using well-organized guerrilla-warfare tactics.

Most of their local efforts focused on cutting the main supply lines to the Romans. They repeatedly attacked supply convoys, and the Romans were unable to develop an effective defence against these attacks.

Their intimate knowledge of the terrain undoubtedly gave Celtiberians and Lusitanians an advantage in battle: this same knowledge would later aid the Asturians and Cantabrians. This advantage was successfully used especially when ambushing Roman forces. These well-organized operations, sometimes made by thousands of warriors, were a sign of a highly-skilled military force with a clear chain of command. These tactics were not characteristic of groups of warriors lacking in military knowledge that had randomly gathered in 'gangs', as they were called by the Romans.

The picture revealed at this stage is very clear. After 200 years of fighting in Hispania, the many reforms implemented in the Roman army and the involvement of the greatest commanders-in-chief of the time – from Scipio Africanus and Cato the Elder in the first chapters of the wars, through Scipio Aemilianus in the most difficult chapters, to Agrippa who completed the conquest of Hispania – had produced neither a military solution nor a dedicated military plan against guerrilla warfare. At first the Romans disparaged this type of warfare and eventually learned, but only after suffering heavy losses, to respect the validity of this method of attack.

Enemy's Warfare Tactics: Fighting according to conventions

Researchers tend to highlight the guerrilla-warfare tactic employed by Hispanic peoples against the Romans. However, the analysis of the sources and archaeological findings reveal a different story. When the conditions were favourable, these peoples preferred to confront the Roman army in head-on battles. Although they were inferior to the Romans in terms of discipline, logistics and command they were capable of operating as an organized army. The analysis of the ancient sources, and especially of the weapons found inside the tombs of the warriors, helps us to conclude that the powerful Hispanic peoples – the Lusitanians and Celtiberians (on which I will focus this time) – used the same weapons as the Romans. This reinforces the claim that their fighting methods were similar. This was to make a direct influence over the use of Hispanic weapons by the Roman army.

In modern historical writings in general, and of Spain in particular, there was a tendency to emphasize and focus on the heroic aspect of the Celtiberian warrior. Much has been said about the 'freedom fighter' using guerrilla warfare, always small numbered as opposed to the great, organized Roman army. This was despite much evidence in the sources concerning the Celtiberian and other armies, who repeatedly fought against Roman armies in head-on battles. This tendency began changing in the 1990s with the publication of new historical research, and the result of archaeological digs.

Since then, the view of Celtiberian warfare has undergone a change; the definition today is not of 'groups of guerrilla fighters', but rather of native armies that did not hesitate to enter into direct confrontation with the Romans.

We will see the evidence, which proves that the Celtiberians preferred conventional fighting to guerrilla warfare throughout the period between the Roman war against the Carthaginians in Hispania and the Numantine war.

However, it can be said that the manner in which the Celtiberians and Lusitanians understood the war was different from the Romans. The Iberian armies differed from the Roman armies in terms of logistics, organization, discipline and the number of fighting men. Their disadvantages in these areas, and especially the fact that they were not united, indicates that despite many victories the Iberians had little chance of defeating Rome in the long run.

On a basic level, i.e. in terms of the fighting prowess of their warriors, the quality of their weapons, and their tactics the differences were much smaller. The method of fighting for both sides was based on the use of the throwing spear and the sword. Descriptions of the battles between the opposing armies during the conquest support this claim. Several ancient sources consider the Romans' ability to position 'fresh soldiers' in the first row, to replace those exhausted in the fighting, as the greatest advantage in any battle, in Hispania and elsewhere.

In the year 207, after the battle between M. Junius Silanus and Mago the Carthaginian, Livius recounts that the Romans had an army of 13,000 infantry soldiers and 500 horsemen. The Carthaginians fielded a force of 9,000 newly-recruited Celtiberian warriors, of these 4,000 were *scutati*.[30] Livius in his account of the battle writes that it was possible to detect between the lines several important details relating to the fighting methods of the Celtiberian warriors.

Firstly, it appears that the 4,000 *scutati* fought a defensive battle against twice the number of Roman legionnaries. Secondly, they fought in an organized row with weapons and methods similar to those used by the Romans. Each *scutati* carried a *scutum* shield for self-defence and probably threw *pila* and *soliferum* spears, before finally engaging the Romans in hand-to-hand combat with a sword. Thirdly, Livius emphasized (twice) that the Celtiberian warriors had been *Novi milites*, *tirones* (new recruits), and yet they fought in an organized formation (contrary to the earlier accepted belief as to the proficiency of the 'barbarian' fighting method). Finally, we can deduce from this account that it was actually the Romans who fought better when engaged in close combat. The Roman advantage in numbers helped them win. Despite the fact that a Roman soldier's equipment was much heavier than that of a Celtiberian warrior, they had an advantage when fighting in small groups. Quesada claims that the Romans were less worried about maintaining organized rows, and fought within the *manipules* to crush the enemy's formations. Newly recruited Celtiberian warriors probably did not know how to fight against the *manipules* or in close combat against a trained legionnaire.

Livius who wrote about the battle of Ampuriae, between the Ilergetes and the army of Cato, during the year 195, describes the Ilerget attack by using the same terms that he used for describing the fighting methods of the Roman armies.[31]

Unlike the fighting method, based on crowded rows of warriors that form the phalanx, used at that time by the different Hellenistic armies in the east, the infantry soldiers from the Hispanic tribes, like their Roman counterparts, fought in more open and flexible rows. The Romans always maintained a high level of discipline within the rows.

Livius recounts that in the year 185, there was a battle between the opposing armies in Carpantia, near Toletum (Toledo). Clashes had taken place between Roman soldiers seeking food and local warriors, and these grew into an all-out battle in which the *praetors* C. Calpurnius and Laeius Quintus were defeated with the loss of 5,000 soldiers. In addition, they were forced to evacuate their camp and retreat. At first light on the next day, the Carpathians approached the Roman camp in battle formation but found it deserted. However, the Romans had left behind a vast number of weapons which the Carpathians collected for probable use in later wars against the Romans.

From this we can learn that the local tribes and the Romans probably used the same weapons: the Romans adopted Hispanic types such as the *Gladius Hispaniensis*, and the local tribes adopted Roman weapons. It can be assumed that this was the quickest way for the tribes to fill their shortage of weapons. This is also why a large number of weapons of Italian origin are found during the excavation of numerous Celtiberian tombs. This does not necessarily mean that the buried persons were allies of the Romans; they could equally be Celtiberian warriors who used the weapon which had been taken from the enemy.

Once the *praetors* C. Calpurnius and Laeius Quintus recovered from their defeat in Carpantia, they set out on another battle against the enemy (it is unclear whether it was only the Carpathians or a coalition of Celtiberians and others). They placed their finest units, the 5th and 7th legions, in the centre of the battle formation. The local army attacked the centre of the Roman rows in an organized and powerful manner and for a long period these attacks endangered the rows of the veteran legionnaires. Only attacks by Roman cavalry on the flanks of the enemy forces saved the Romans, and eventually brought about a victory. In the year 181, a war broke out again in Hispania Citerior. There had been several battles between the native armies, mostly Celtiberians and Roman armies. Livius recounts that the Celtiberians recruited 35,000 new inexperienced soldiers and constructed a fortified camp on a plateau to house them, exactly replicating those built by the Roman army. *Praetor* P. Flaccus, governor of the province, managed to hastily recruit an army, which also included allies, and begin preparations for a battle. The Celtiberians waited in vain, on the plain between the two camps, for the Roman forces to enter the field in their close-battle formation. But the Romans were either not yet ready to fight or were waiting for the right moment.

Flaccus decided to order a night assault behind the enemy's line which was successful and allowed the Romans to set fire to and destroy the Celtiberian camp.

The Celtiberians were not to be discouraged and fiercely counterattacked the Romans. However, the 7th legion returned to the battlefield at the last moment and saved the Romans from defeat.

Once again, this proves that the Celtiberians wanted to fight by exclusively using a frontal assault and then only in daylight, while the Romans were looking for other, creative ways to fight.

There is also evidence that when the Celtiberians found themselves in an inferior position on the battlefield they did not resort to using the tactics of attack and retreat, but imprudently attacked the Romans head-on.

In the year 180, Flaccus was trapped in an ambush which developed into an all-out battle.[32] Livius wrote that when the Celtiberians had felt that they would not be able to break the Roman formations by attacking in organized rows, they attacked in a closed, fist-like formation.[33] This caused great panic in the rows of the Roman army which resulted in their defeat.

The description above deals with a fierce battle between two armies, one of which was more organized than the other. Yet, this does not contradict the fact that an assault in a fist-like formation represents classic military tactics of heavy infantry force and not guerrilla warfare.

A year later in 179, the new *praetor* employed a variety of measures: diplomacy, siege and finally an all-out battle to crush Celtiberian resistance.

Livius speaks of a great battle in the area of Mons Chaunus, Moncão, which took place between the Roman and Celtiberian armies. The battle was not resolved by the end of the day and the Celtiberians returned to their fortified camp for the night. The battle was renewed the next day and after an arduous fight the Roman army was victorious. However, both sides suffered heavy losses.[34]

Between the years 154 and 150, Nobilior led military campaigns to besiege the cities of Segeda and Numantia, who according to Appianus avoided battle in open areas. On 23 August 154, Carus the leader of the warriors of Segeda set an ambush with some 20,000 infantry and 5,000 cavalrymen lying in wait hidden in a forest. Carus waited for his opportunity and attacked the Romans marching in organized rows across the open ground. The ambush was successful and some 6,000 Romans were killed. Later, the Romans counterattacked and stabilized the situation. Carus was killed during this part of the battle. Appianus, who did not really understand military tactics, actually did describe a battle on open ground, which had begun with a large-scale ambush.

A mass of 25,000 warriors, fighting as an organized army where each soldier had a defined role and accepted the authority of command undoubtedly constituted an efficient fighting force.

In the year 143, battles against the Celtiberians were resumed. The military campaign by C. Pompeius in the year 141, ended with a massive battle in which, according to Appianus, both the Celtiberian and Roman armies fighting in organized battle formations fought to a stalemate at nightfall.

An analysis of Appianus' account shows that the Celtiberians had positioned an organized army which had fought conventionally, exactly like the Romans.

The Roman army usually enjoyed a clear advantage over other armies in frontal battles due to their superior organization, their clear chain of command, strict discipline and flexible tactics. One of the reasons why the commanders in the Roman army sometimes ordered agricultural crops to be destroyed and enemy cities and villages plundered was an attempt by them to force the enemy to face them in battle.

The commander-in-chief that headed the Roman army was of crucial importance to the success of the army on the battlefield. So crucial, that he sometimes prevented the annihilation of an entire army by using his military expertise. But even these were not an absolute guarantee to victory on the battlefield.

Successful commanders-in-chief, such as Pyrrhuss, Hannibal or Viriathus, were successful in breaking up the rigidly aligned Roman formations by using leadership skills and tactical expertise, which were superior to their Roman counterparts. During the Roman wars in Hispania there had been countless instances where a Roman army was defeated by a frontal attack, due to a commander's poor judgment in positioning his forces. For example, the Scipio brothers suffered from overconfidence which led to the destruction of a large part of their army by the Carthaginians in the year 211. Inevitably, overconfidence would lead to their deaths during a battle in southern Hispania.

Probably the best example of failed leadership occurred in the year 137, during a battle where consul Mancius led his army into a trap set by the Numantines. In order to save his soldiers from certain death at the hands of the enemy he was forced to surrender. Equally important are the displays of initiative and creativity at all levels of the Roman officer order. By displaying leadership and initiative, the tribune Marcius saved the situation after the two supreme commanders, the Scipio brothers, were killed in battle. He collected together their remaining forces, that were scattered over the battlefield, and led them to safety in an area north of the Ebro which was under Roman control.

Based on the analysis of the various sources and weapons found, it can be concluded that the Celtiberians – as a coalition or alone – fought, when possible, against the Roman armies using a conventional military framework. They fought in open battles, and although they did not operate according to the strict military discipline and highly-organized levels of the Roman army they were by no means a 'band' or a 'gang of robbers', as it had been claimed in the past. The Celtiberians posed a threat to the Roman army countless times, and even won battles on numerous occasions.

The commanders-in-chief of the Roman army, who had extensive military experience and expertise in leadership, were to make the decisions that sealed the fate of their forces, managed the battle to a victory, or attempt to minimize the damage in the event of a defeat.

Expressions of 'unconventional' warfare in archaeological findings

A battlefield is an archaeological site for all intents and purposes, and therefore a research approach should be employed. The site should be identified, surveyed and excavated and the findings carefully interpreted. But due to the different nature of the many sites it is necessary to match the method of work used to study them. The archaeologist must be aware of the different limitations that exist in the research of a site and take them into account in his work.

The first limitation is related to the identification of the site. To date, famous battle sites such as Cannae, Pidna and Zama have not been identified conclusively. Sometimes, there are only a few artefacts to be found in the field. Identification is difficult in the case of a temporary camp which was built from wood, a degradable material.

Canals that were dug and ramparts that were built in order to fortify a camp have also disappeared over the centuries due to climatic conditions, but importantly due to modern infrastructure development – both for agriculture and construction – which damages the stratification of the layers and, consequently, the remains.

The second limitation is associated with the need to locate the boundaries of the battlefield. The average size of a battlefield in ancient times was between ½ and 1½sqkm. At times, it is only an area of several hundred square meters, but sometimes it is a large and even several kilometres long.

In this case, it is very hard to assess the structure and the size of the battlefield and also the forces involved and their movements in the battle. This could lead to miscalculations as to the size of the army, and erroneous comparisons to the written sources.

Another problem arises when there is an attempt to translate the data in the sources to the data in the field. Misinterpretation of the sources, which are used as a complementary tool for understanding the battle, can lead to significant deviations in the different calculations. However, we can still use the data that appears in the written sources, if it is used wisely and carefully. We know, for example, that the Republican army, which consisted of *centurias* and *manipules*, used to position a formation of four to eight soldier rows deep. Therefore, a *centuria* could operate with only five to seven soldiers in the front row. This diminished the battle formation of the legion significantly, and had far-reaching implications on the size of the forces that could operate in a certain battlefield.

The third limitation lies in the unique character of a battlefield as an archaeological site. On an 'ordinary' site, it is possible to track the chronological development, by studying the different layers, the differences in architecture and the immense evolution seen in the different findings. However, on a battlefield time stood still and artefacts left by the two armies, after the fighting, remained in place.

It is possible to discover weapons and other military equipment which belong to other periods or regions. There is no way of knowing when and how the armies obtained their equipment, especially when we are dealing with armies that were based on the spoils of war, such as the Celtiberian and Lusitanian.

The fourth limitation lies in the small amount of equipment in general, and weapons in particular, which were left on the battlefield. Combat equipment was very valuable, since to produce it required special skills, and most of the equipment was taken from the battlefield, by the triumphant army, as soon as the battle was over. Only the battered equipment or that which was not collected by the victors was left on the battlefield. The surveyor or archaeologist has a better chance of finding military equipment on the perimeter of a battlefield. For instance, places where defeated soldiers hid, or where the wounded were taken for treatment and military burial grounds are worth investigating.

The fifth limitation is associated with the confusion that prevails among soldiers during battle, and its implications on the reliability of evidence relating to a certain battle. Anyone who is a battle researcher or has certain military training knows that the warrior remembers very little of events in a battle, this is why the individual involved sees it from his unique point of view, which is sometimes different to the overall picture of the battle.

An archaeologist, who relies on historical resources for the interpretation of the material findings, must keep in mind that these sources should be treated with great scepticism. In cases when the sources are written by a commander-in-chief, such as Julius Caesar, or an historian, such as Polybius (who wrote about the story of Scipio Aemilianus) it should be taken into account that the narratives are biased, and were usually intended to praise and pay tribute to the commander-in-chief.

It should be obvious that evidence from the battlefield must be treated as a piece in a jig-saw puzzle which only when completed can provide the overall picture of the battle.

Apart from those specified above, there is an additional limitation related to the understanding of the army and battlefield, and this is the temporary camp. The Romans were not the only ones who built temporary camps, which would serve their army during the long marches. The Greeks, Carthaginians and Celtiberians also built temporary camps. The latter built temporary fortified camps and surrounded them with ramparts. Most of these camps were built of degradable material, mainly wood, which does not last overtime in the Mediterranean weather conditions. Therefore, in many cases, the only evidence of these are the remains of the fortifications, which are usually the only available material dating parameter, which can be also used to understand the layout and the number soldiers that could be housed in its confines. However, this also appears to be a difficult issue.

It is not recommended for example, to draw a sweeping comparison between the findings in the field and the description of the camp in the sources (Polybius, Frontinus or Vegetius), since the size of the camp was dependent not only on the number of soldiers it housed, but also on the number of horses that were used by the cavalry. This means that it is impossible to rely on the results of a common statistical equation to calculate the number of soldiers per square meter. As previously mentioned, there are additional parameters that can make it even more difficult to calculate the size, such as the topography of the location, also the construction and number of internal buildings.

It is impossible to avoid statistical calculations based on the size and extent of a camp. But the results must not be accepted as the absolute truth; they should be cross-referenced, where possible, with other data such as pottery, bones of animals used for food or transport, or the existence of a bakery or metal workshops discovered inside the camp or in its vicinity.

The study of a camp can also assist in understanding the battlefield. For example, if we have two camps in close proximity that had belonged to different armies and we know the location of their source of water – a spring, stream, cistern or well – then, if the historical sources specify the distance between the camp and the water source, it is possible to make an approximation of where the battle was fought.

The sources inform that many times, the bodies of the dead from the defeated army were left on the field once the battle was over. Human remains and personal equipment, not necessarily weapons, have remained scattered on the field for centuries. The findings from the burial fields are of great value for completing the picture of the armies that fought on these battlefields. Much of the military equipment was taken from the battlefield and is sometimes discovered in a tomb; unfortunately many have been looted over time. In terms of archaeology, the weapons and military equipment found in tombs are the most important items for completing the picture described in the written sources, and sometimes disprove them.

The most obvious thing when studying Hispanic tombs is that the type of weapons and military equipment discovered can be identified, which strengthens the claim that the Celtiberians and other Hispanic peoples fought as part of a regular army. These collections include a large number of swords and spears, also personal protection equipment, such as armour and metal helmets. However, arrowheads and metal billets, which are characteristic of raids, are rarely found. These collections are no different from those discovered in cemeteries used by the Romans or any other Hellenistic army, and quite convincingly confirm the existence of an organized army.

The open battlefield represents a specific combat concept, which is very different from another type of combat, the siege. The different types of siege have provided a wealth of archaeological remains, and play an important role in the study of how the army performed during both offensive and defensive operations.

It should be noted that ancient sources provide little evidence to describe the way the Roman army used its war machines in Hispania. There are rare descriptions of the use of siege machines. This lack of information can be resolved, though not fully, by using the wealth of archaeological findings by researchers from the second half of the twentieth century to the present day.

Quesada claims that the small quantity of findings relating to siege battles proves that there were barely any actions of this type, until at least the second century. He also says that the Iberians did not build complex fortifications, apart from several instances (Saguntum, Numantia, and Segeda). This is due to the fact that these peoples believed in 'active defence', if an enemy surrounded their settlement or attacked, they would come out and attack. But there are remains that confirm the use of artillery in siege battles.

Several partially-preserved catapults and catapult stones have been discovered in Spain and prove that Roman armies used these throughout the conquest of Hispania, from the end of the third century until the second half of the first century.

The findings also illustrate the development of the siege defence methods, as a counter-response to the emergence of the Roman war machines. The Iberian fortification was a relatively simple construction. Usually, these consisted of a tower built inside the settlement and a simple brick or stone perimeter wall surrounded by a moat. In the course of the second century, they started digging double and triple moats, as well as building more towers. The width of the moat increased from 4 to 8m to 20 to 25m. This was done in order to keep Roman artillery as far away as possible. According to Appianus, Aemilianus used many siege machines and also built many two-storey siege towers around the entire fortifications of Numantia.

'Scorpio' catapults and *ballista* were placed in these towers. Archaeological findings enable cross-reference with the data from the sources. The results of surveys and excavations inside siege camp Number 3 at Gran Atalaya, show that it was defended by twenty-seven towers many of which were fitted with a ramp, probably for the purpose of raising an artillery machine.

The remains of Scorpio catapults were discovered in Ampurias, Gerona, in a layer which dated to the first half of the second century.

Metal parts of a catapult were discovered in an area of 915sqm at Teruel, Aragon. This site has been dated to the end of the second century, and was destroyed in the years 72 to 80, during the revolt by Sertorius.

In addition to these artillery machines, several ammunition stores were also discovered. These were spread over a wide area in the central and northern Hispania, and were dated especially to the period from the middle of the second century until the 70s of the first century (from the Celtiberian wars until the war with Sertorius), although they first appeared as early as the end of the third century.

The numerous and long wars and sieges of Numantia, which took place between the years 154 and 133, contribute significantly to the understanding of siege battles in the time of the Roman conquest of Hispania. The tendency of the archaeological research is to focus on the economic, social and psychological burden that these wars posed on Rome. Numantia is, naturally, the richest site for ammunition findings, due to the large-scale siege laid on the city. It is known from the works of Appianus, that the army of Scipio Aemilianus surrounded Numantia. Scipio used scores of artillery pieces during the siege; the large number of stone balls discovered in excavations at the main camp of Aemilianus is evidence of a significant use of artillery.

At a site excavated near Zaragoza, identified as the Celtiberian city of Contrebia, numerous stone balls used as ammunition for the *ballista* were discovered. The skeleton of a boy, who had been beheaded, was also discovered. Archaeologists believe that this boy was hit by a stone ball from a *ballista*. The dating process of the stone balls is not straightforward, due to the destruction of many layers at the site; the earliest are dated to the wars between 190 and 151. The settlement was then rebuilt, but destroyed again in the mid-70s of the first century, during the war with Sertorius. The settlement was rebuilt, but destroyed again in the 30s of the first century.

At the fortress of Espina del Gallego, located in the north of the Cantabrian Mountains, the head of a *pilum catapultarium* (iron catapult sling) was found wedged between the stones of the fortification. This finding indicates that the fortress had been conquered following a Roman siege. The discovery of a coin dates the conquest of the site to the Cantabrian wars.

The earliest Roman camp in Hispania was discovered by Schulten in Almenara, 9km north of the site identified as Saguntum, the walls of which were preserved. It is accepted practice to date the camp to the journey made by the Scipio brothers, in the year 217, along the coast on their way to Saguntum.

Additional early camps which were discovered are dated to the first half of the second century: Renieblas, associated with the military campaign of P. Nobilior against Numantia, and the camp in Pinia Redonda, associated with the military campaign by Scipio Aemilianus against Numantia.

Polybius wrote that the Scipio brothers built a camp of forty *stadia* in Saguntum, adjacent to the temple of Aphrodite. The camp was trapezoidal in shape and measured: 500m from both equal sides, and 300 and 200m on the other two sides. The wall was 1.20m wide and sixteen towers were positioned along its length.

Over the years, the Romans built many camps. Most were temporary about which there is no information. However as previously stated, in recent years quite a number of permanent camps have been or are being excavated.

These camps were shaped and of similar size to those described in Polybius' sixth book, which according to Frontinus had become standard since the war against Pyrrhus, in the first half of the third century.

The last camp, Layer 3 at the Gran Atalaya site is the largest; some 25,000 soldiers would have been housed in this camp: two legions, including Italian allies and Iberian auxiliary forces.

The largest concentration of Roman army camps from the period of the Republic in Hispania, and perhaps the entire Roman Empire, are to be found at Meseta Castellana in the central northern part of the Iberian Peninsula. In this area, many army camps have been discovered and studied, most of which are associated with the Celtiberian war (154 to 133), and were the first to be excavated by Schulten. Two of these, which are considered to be the earliest, are dated to the wars that Cato waged in the year 195, and three are dated to 135 to 130 and the Numantine war. These are probably the camps of Scipio Aemilianus.

Chapter Five

Changes the Roman Army has undergone following the Hispanic Wars

In this chapter, I will analyze the changes that the Roman army had undergone, as a consequence of 200 years of war to conquer the Iberian Peninsula, and focus on three fundamental topics: weapons, structure of a legion and ways of exercising power.

Also to be discussed is the process by which the Roman army adopted weapons from Hispania, as well as a variety of issues arising from this process: were these weapons adopted in their original form, or have they been modified by the Romans; was the adoption of weapons a direct or indirect result of the Hispanic wars and when had this process begun; finally, why were weapons from Hispania in particular, were adopted by the Roman army. Later on, the significant changes that took place in the Roman army will be addressed, including the most important one: the move from a legion based on *manipules* to one based on *cohorts*. It has been claimed that the Hispanic wars played a very important role in this process, although there is no reference to this issue in ancient sources. However, an analysis of archaeological findings plays a major role in the conclusions drawn in this chapter.

Adoption of weapons of Hispanic origin

In the final third of the third century, during the Second Punic War, and the first decades of the second century the Roman army underwent a process of adopting new weapons that originated from armies that they had fought in different regions. New types of swords, spears and daggers, apparently originating from Hispania, became standard weapons in a Roman legion at the end of the period of the Republic and the early Empire.

Out of these three weapons, only with the *gladius hispaniensis* do archaeological findings concur with historical sources regarding the Hispanic origin of this weapon.

The *pugium* (dagger), which appears in a Roman context in archaeological excavations, is not found in the historical sources as a weapon that was adopted during the Hispanic wars. Finally, the data regarding the spear is inconclusive, both in archaeological findings and in historical resources, which contain many contradictions regarding this issue.

In order to explain the possible adoption of weapons of Hispanic origin by the Roman army one must refer to a broader issue: the similarity between Roman and Hispanic fighting techniques. As detailed in Chapter 4, there are many similarities between the methods of warfare between the Roman armies and those from the Celtiberian world. This similarity does not exist between the Roman armies and those from the Hellenistic.

A Roman tactical grouping based on *manipules* could not fight for example, the Hellenistic *sarissa* without significantly altering its military formation which basically, changed a Roman legion into a new type of *phalange*, and return to the time of a Roman *phalange* of the fifth century.

If the adoption of a weapon of Hispanic origin went smoothly, then by adopting a Hellenistic formation the Roman army would be transformed into a less versatile and inferior military force.

In fact, the Roman legionnaire, like the Hispanic infantry soldier, fought using heavy throwing weapons (*pilum*, *soliferum*) and a sword which required a reasonable space to wield.

When comparing the Roman and Macedonian armies, historical sources address the many differences between them, both in terms of weapons and fighting techniques. However, when these sources refer to Hispanic armies, and mainly focus on the ethics of the leaders or their military capabilities – usually flawed, as far as the sources are concerned – they call them 'bandit leaders' or *duces latrones* ('thieves leaders').

However, when the sources describe the battles between Roman and Hispanic armies they see no difference in the type of soldier, but concentrate on the issue of ethics and the differences in education between the Roman warrior and the barbaric Hispanic. It should also be noted that some of the weapons that the Romans adopted in Hispania were of Gaelic origin. However, the Romans did not embrace the Gaelic versions of these weapons when they had first came into contact with these weapons as early as the Gaelic invasion in the year 386. However, the Montefortino helmet was accepted and became, from the beginning of the fourth century, a standard item of military equipment throughout Italy. The helmet was probably first adopted by the Etruscans, as an example was discovered in tombs dating to the fourth century.

Another factor that affected the adoption of Hispanic weapons was supply. The requirements of an army fighting far from home for a lengthy period, sometimes years, required the creation of new solutions. These included the fabrication of weapons within the legion, an action that would become the standard at the time of the Empire, as well as using weapons captured from the Hispanic armies or the purchase from the local craftsmen.

When the Roman army was formed for the campaign in Hispania the weapons and equipment were brought from Italy. The problem arose when it was required to urgently renew the inventory following prolonged military action far away from Italy. It became necessary to find a source of manufacture and supply nearby, thus avoiding a lengthy delay for delivery from a distant Italy. The adoption of Hispanic weapons can therefore be considered as another component in the process of the Roman armies' adjustment to the issue of supply that arose during the wars.

Cato, who had believed in the policy of *bellum se ipsum alet* (self-sufficiency), initiated the process of exploiting local resources, and was his way of obtaining regular, and reliable, supplies in the regions in which his forces operated.

Ransom payment and the levying of taxes were also used as another way of acquiring different supplies, including weapons.

It should be noted that the transfer of weapons and other supplies between the Roman armies and local tribes was a two-way process based on the outcome of fighting between the two sides. According to Florus, after the Celtiberians had defeated the Romans in a battle, they demanded that Mancinus order his army to surrender their weapons. This interesting case illustrates that the mutual influences between the two armies, which include the adoption of weapons, is also manifested in the archaeological findings and also recognized by ancient Roman literary sources.

I will now examine archaeological and historical evidence, concerning the possible Hispanic origin of the three weapons mentioned above, that became the characteristic weapons for the Roman army in the late Republic period and early Empire: the *pilum*, *gladius* and *pugio*.

Adolf Schulten, the German archaeologist, was the first to suggest, quite decisively, that the Romans had adopted the *pilum* from Hispania. This was a heavy weapon that the legionnaires threw, just before entering into hand-to-hand combat, their main objective was to cause chaos within the enemy lines and disrupt their battle formation. Julius Caesar provides an excellent example of how the *pilum* was used to disrupt the Gaelic army's plan, basically by smashing their shields. Caesar describes how a salvo of *pila* had forced them to dispose of the shields and fight unprotected. According to Polybius, the *pilum* was a weapon with a great penetration capability, and could penetrate an enemy's shield and body armour. Polybius also notes that the *pilum* could be used for close combat. An accurate replica of the weapon made by Connolly weighed 1.35kg.

There is quite a lot of confusion in different Greek and Roman sources regarding the origin of the *pilum* which became standard

Tomb 13 at Cerro Balas.
A variety of Roman Weaponry in Quesada Gladius XX, *2000, Page 194.*

equipment for the Roman army. In fact, it can be concluded that the Romans had absolutely no idea as to the origin of the weapon.

For decades and centuries, at least since the time of the Samnite wars in the fourth century, the Romans used different throwing weapons which changed overtime due to different external influences. When writing of the origin of the first *pilum* used by the Romans, Diodorus Siculus states that they had been impressed by the quality of the spears and shields used by the Samnite, and decided to adopt them and became experts in using these weapons.

Today, we can safely say that based on archaeological findings, the Romans had different metal-shafted throwing weapons with fine arrowhead-shaped points. These weapons can be generically called *pilum* and were used by Roman armies in all the regions throughout the Mediterranean.

The *falarica* (Hispanic *pilum*) probably originated in Gaul where it was known as *gaesum*. It was brought from Gaul to central Hispania and then to Italy, possibly with various changes being made during this period. In Italy, the weapon was called *pilum*. Therefore, it can be

References to the 'Spanish gladius' in the sources

Source	Reference	Events described
Suda (tenth century AD)		Adoption of the *gladius* by the Romans
Polybius	2,30-33	The battle of Telemon against the Gauls, in the year 225
Polybius	3,114,2-4	The battle of Cannae, in the year 216
Polybius	6,23,6	Probably refers to the war against Hannibal (Wallbank 1957, p 703)
Livius	7,10,5	Events in the fourth century
Livius	22,26,5	The battle of Cannae, in the year 216
Livius	31,34	The war against the Kingdom of Macedonia, the end of the third century
Livius	38,21,13	The war against the Gauls, in the year 189

concluded that Schulten's theory as to the origin of the Roman *pilum* is not reinforced by archaeological findings. The basis for this theory is found in description of the Saguntian *falarica* by Livius, who states that the origin of the Roman *pilum* is the Hispanic *falarica*, probably from the middle of the third century. It can equally be deduced that the familiar Roman *pilum* of the second to third century AD is the result of the evolution of the Italian *pilum* which originated from Gaul. Over time this was influenced by similar weapons, including the Celtiberian *falcate*, the Romans encountered in their military campaigns in many different regions.

The increasing number of Roman swords dating to the second and first centuries being discovered in Spain, are different from the Imperial short-bladed sword (such as the Mainz and Pompeii type) and shed new light on the question of the Hispanic origin of the 'Spanish *gladius*'. These findings indicate that there is a clear correlation with the 'La Tene I' sword which was adopted by the Celtiberians in the fourth century. The later version was used by the Celtiberian armies, who fought the Romans at the end of the third century.

It is worth mentioning that although there had been stylistic changes to the shaft and sword decorations, the length of the blade remained unchanged. In Gaul, as time moved on, the blade was lengthened as it evolved into a completely different sword.

The evolution of the *gladius* began at the dawn of the second century, as a fine-bladed sword some 65cm in length. Towards the end of the century it is lengthened by 4 to 5cm, and remains this length until the end of the first century.

The only text that specifically mentions the adoption of the Iberian sword by the Romans is in the *Suda*, a Byzantine lexicon composed in the tenth century AD. The relevant paragraph reads: '…The Celtiberian sword was much better than the other swords… Therefore the Romans, after the war against Hannibal, abandoned their swords and adopted the Iberian sword instead…'

References to the 'Spanish gladius' in the sources

Polybius was the earliest historical source to mention a Spanish sword used by the Romans. When he describes the weapons of the *hastati* in the second century, he mentions a 'Spanish sword' that was carried on the waist.

The sword had a very strong double-edged blade and could be used for thrusting and slashing movements. Polybius, like Livius, mentions a short sword used mainly for stabbing and cutting carried by the Iberian warriors in Hannibal's army.

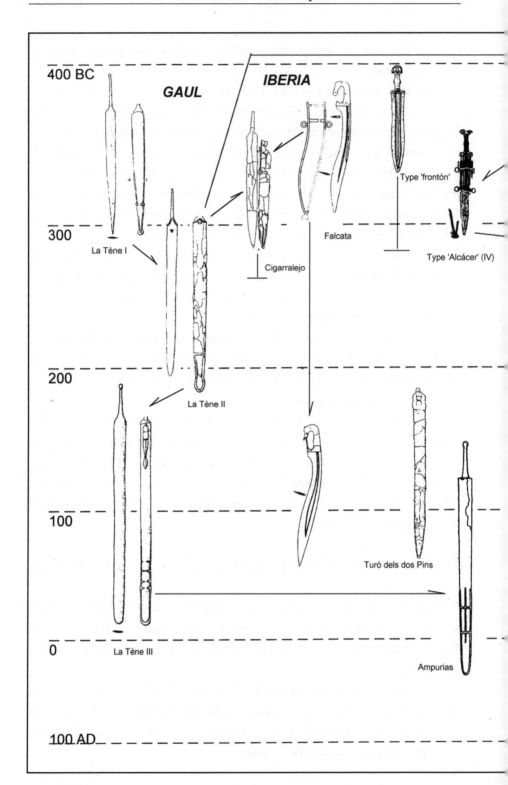

400 BC

GAUL   *IBERIA*

Type 'frontón'

300

La Tène I

Falcata

Type 'Alcácer' (IV)

Cigarralejo

200

La Tène II

Turó dels dos Pins

100

0

La Tène III

Ampurias

100 AD

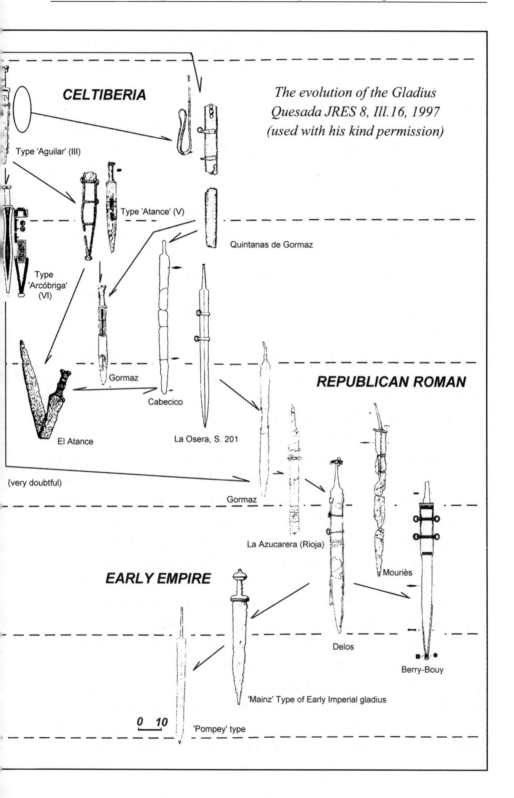

CELTIBERIA

The evolution of the Gladius
Quesada JRES 8, Ill.16, 1997
(used with his kind permission)

Type 'Aguilar' (III)

Type 'Atance' (V)

Quintanas de Gormaz

Type 'Arcóbriga' (VI)

Gormaz

Cabecico

REPUBLICAN ROMAN

El Atance

La Osera, S. 201

(very doubtful)

Gormaz

La Azucarera (Rioja)

Mouriès

EARLY EMPIRE

Delos

Berry-Bouy

0 10

'Mainz' Type of Early Imperial gladius

'Pompey' type

They also indicate the difference between this and the much longer Gaelic sword: '... the blade of the Spanish sword was made especially for stabbing, whereas the Gaelic sword was used only for cutting, and that required a lot of effort.'

Therefore, we can agree with the conclusions drawn by Quesada and Connolly: the first is that at the end of the third century the Iberians had developed and used the short sword, while the Gaelic still used the 'La Tene II' long sword. The second is that the Romans had encountered the Spanish sword prior to the conquest of Hispania.

In conclusion, it can be said that the Spanish *gladius* originates from the Celtiberian sword which evolved from the 'La Tene I', which underwent changes in Hispania and was adopted by the Roman army, between the battle of Cannae (216) and the conquest of New Carthage (209) during the Second Punic War. Quesada and Carter believe that the latter date is more accurate.

The *gladius* was used as a standard sword by all Roman legions throughout the *Principate* period. During the period of the Late Empire, it was replaced by the *Spatha*, a longer single-edged sword, which had previously been used by their auxiliary forces.

The Hispanic source of the Roman *pugio* (dagger) remains questionable and even quite the opposite from that of the *pilum*. There is no reference to the *pugio* in ancient sources, but there is archaeological evidence that points to Hispania as the almost certain source of this weapon. Daggers even slightly similar to the legionnaire's *pugio*, other than the Celtiberian dagger, have not been discovered in other locations during recent archaeological research. The daggers uncovered at sites such as Herrera de Pisuerga, Palencia, and Cáceres El Viejo, clearly have features seen on later Roman daggers dating from the first to third centuries AD and were in use throughout the Empire.

The Celtiberian dagger probably entered the Roman military's inventory during the Numantine War, in the middle of the second century (possibly at the beginning) as noted by Ulbert, Quesada and Connolly. Ulbert suggests that it was first taken as spoils of war. The process of the adoption of this weapon continued for many years, before it became part of the Roman inventory at the time of Augustus.

Quesada believes that Roman officers and a number of soldiers were the first to use the weapon, possibly attracted by its aesthetic beauty. Over the years, the Celtiberian dagger evolved and was adopted by the Roman army in the first century as part of a legionnaire's standard equipment.

Structural changes in the army: the transition to permanent armies and legions

The Roman army underwent extensive changes during the first and second centuries. These changes transformed the army: in the years 16 to 17 the army with which Agrippa conquered Asturia and Cantabria was completely different to the army which Scipio Africanus commanded in his war against Hannibal at the end of the third century.

The process of transformation, which began in the second century, gained momentum at the time of G. Marius and ended with Augustus, who transformed it from an army of volunteers into a professional army. This new army was formed of permanent legions and based on *cohorts* instead of *manipules*, and the State provided new types of weapons. The commanders, who headed the army in distant areas of conflict, once enjoyed a high level of autonomy and quite often operated on their own, independent from Rome. Experience gained in the Hispanic Wars most certainly played a very important role in this transformation.

Roman triumphs in wars beginning at the end of the third century until the first half of the second century (Second Punic War in the west, and the wars in the east against the Greeks, also the Macedonian and Seleucid kingdoms) resulted in Roman dominance over vast and distant territories. Territories such as Hispania, Greece, Macedonia, the many islands (in the east and west of the Mediterranean) and also Asia Minor were absorbed, whether directly or indirectly into the Roman state. A result of the conquest was to force the Romans to make extensive changes to the structure of their army.

In most of these areas, the Romans were forced, for the first time, to station permanent legions. This led to a growing autonomy for the governors and army commanders, up to the point of them becoming independent; if not '*de jure*', then '*de facto*'.

This was particularly evident in Hispania. At the beginning of the second century, Cato who commanded the army operating in Hispania initiated the process of reducing the dependence on Rome. Cato preferred to purchase locally produced items and farm produce which was plentiful and available. This was supplied to the Roman army under agreements with the different tribes or if necessary taken by force.

The arrival of supplies in sufficient quantities and within a reasonable period of time was very much dependent on the mood of the Senate in Rome. However, the Senate did not always agree with their commander regarding the state of affairs in Hispania. This was due to the lack of information being received or a lack of political support for the commanders among the ruling circles in the Senate. Moreover, there was the risk incurred by transporting supplies by sea, as most were to Hispania, due to weather conditions and currents across the Mediterranean Sea.

Another important innovation for the Roman army at the end of the Republic period was the emergence of the permanent legions. The long and distant wars in the Iberian Peninsula of the second and first centuries can be considered as the main reason for their introduction.

Long-term service in the same military unit produced an *esprit de corps* and the evolving of traditions. Clear evidence of this can be seen, as early as the 50s of the first century, in the army of Julius Caesar during the Gaelic wars. Throughout the many wars there are references to the names of the legions, as well as to the pride felt by the serving soldiers.

Particularly prominent are the many references relating to the 10th Legion, the *Legio X Equestris* ('cavalry legion') in the Gaelic war. The first: the 10th Legion, led by the brave bearer of the eagle, headed the invasion by Julius Caesar's army into Great Britain. When the soldiers were frightened to get off their boats on the coast and make contact with the barbarians, the brave bearer of the eagle jumped into the water and charged the enemy with the standard of the legion in his hands. This way, he said, he would fulfil his duty to the Republic and to his commander (Julius Caesar).[35] Thus, the bearer of the standard collected other forces of the legion and headed the attack. Another important reference relates to the battle of Gergovia: following a hasty attack on the city of Gergovia, when Gaelic forces drove the Romans out of their town Julius Caesar then sent the 10th Legion to block the Gaelic attack and force them back behind the walls of the city.[36] In addition to the 10th Legion, Julius Caesar often mentions other legions by name in his writings.

By the end of the second century, little is left of the army that Polybius describes in his sixth book in the middle of that century. Goldsworthy wrote: 'The Roman army has turned into a professional regular army, which proved a significant advantage over most of its enemies.' A new legion in the first century is now formed of *cohorts* instead of single *manipules*.

The *manipules* no longer operate independently, but as groups of three: the *manipule* of *hastate*, the *manipule* of *Principes* and the *manipule* of *triarii* to form a *cohort*. A legion was formed of ten *manipules*. The manipular legion was designed for the wars of the past, in which great battles would determine the outcome. In the new wars which were mostly fought, in battles on a much smaller scale, against barbarian tribes the original style of legion lacked flexibility.

In most of the wars fought during the last centuries of the period of the Republic and the beginning of the *Principate*, Roman armies fought against inferior enemies which were less developed in terms of discipline and organization. These were one-sided wars, in which a 'regular' army' (the Roman army) fought against an enemy which used 'irregular' methods. At the beginning of the last century in Europe, these were called 'small wars'. Their objective was conquest, punishment and the deterrence or suppression of revolts. A legion consisting of ten *cohorts* would function as the 'manipular legion' in a large battle, but it would be flexible enough to fight in a small-scale war. This was due to the fact that each *cohort* had its own commander, allowing it to operate autonomously as a smaller-scale legion. A unit consisting of several hundred soldiers could perform tasks which *manipules* were too small to perform, and a legion too large and unmanoeuvrable.

Cadiou claims that the transition from the *manipular* to the *cohort* legion was completed only after the civil wars of the second half of the second century, and that until then the *cohorts* were used as a specific solution to urgent situations on the battlefield. The example he provides to establish his case is a battle of the Jugurthine war fought in the year 108, when Metellus managed to save his army from defeat by using the *cohort*. In fact, this event clearly demonstrates the supremacy of the *cohort* on the battlefield. Metellus was aware of this supremacy and therefore, Cadiou is wrong in claiming that Metellus did not find his solution 'out of the blue', but rather that the *cohort* was already part of his army. A *cohort* was the correct size to perform a wide array of tasks that the Roman army had found difficult during the Hispanic wars: punishment duties, collecting supplies, marching through narrow and winding valleys, and pursuing a fleeing enemy from the battlefield. Also a *cohort* was used to consolidate the territory following a triumph in the battle.

As mentioned in previous chapters, the last two tasks were particularly problematic for the Romans since their enemies, and particularly the Lusitanians, used deception when 'fleeing' from the battle..

Most of these tasks would end with disaster for the Romans, as in the year 151 when Galba recklessly pursued Viriathus and lost 7,000 of his soldiers, half of his army.

If the commanders of the Roman army had flexible, powerful and fast units, i.e. *cohorts* at that time, they would have been able to respond proportionally and not endanger their forces in pursuit, usually in vain, of a faked enemy retreat. The issue of holding an occupied territory was also a problem for the Romans. There is no doubt that they did not have sufficient manpower which would allow them to distribute their legions effectively throughout Hispania and build fortifications wherever necessary. However, it was possible to scatter a legion of ten *cohorts* over a large area, each capable of working as an autonomous force, and maintain a fortified camp.

At first a *cohort* contained 480 soldiers divided into six *centurias* of eighty soldiers each commanded by a centurion. In the first half of the first century, the first *cohort* in every legion was increased to 800 soldiers, divided into five *centurias* of 160 soldiers. The first *cohort* became an 'elite unit', which guarded the legion standard.

Despite the importance of these *cohorts*, no holder of a formal position was placed above the commander, usually a veteran centurion, of these units.

These changes in the composition of a legion provided the army commanders with a better ability to provide a rapid and efficient response to any unexpected situations. These means had not been previously available to commanders in Hispania. Julius Caesar had succeeded numerous times to react quickly and efficiently against rebellious tribes in Gaul without having to make special preparations. This is how the Romans acted in the first century AD at the time of the *Principate*, or when Cato operated in Britain in the year 60 AD during the revolt by Boadicea, or in the year 66 when Florus was in action during the Jewish rebellion in Judea. These two commanders acted rapidly and used a relatively small force in order to provide an adequate response until the main army arrived on the battlefield.

There is no doubt that one of the major factors which contributed to the transformation of the Roman army, was the reforms attributed to G. Marius. These were initiated, to a large extent, by his personal experiences gathered in the Numidic, Cimbrian and Teutonic wars he had fought in at the end of the second century. However, it is possible to also identify the influence of the Hispanic wars over these reforms. Therefore, Bell is correct when he claims that the *cohort*-based legion appeared in Hispania in the second century following a long process of reviewing the fighting tactics used on the battlefield.

Marius was not the creator of the new legion, but one of its founders. Cadiou is wrong in claiming that there is no link between Hispania and the origin of the *cohorts*.

Cadiou bases his arguments on the limited knowledge available on the fighting methods of the Cimbrian, Teutones and Hispanic tribes, since ancient sources have omitted any descriptions of fighting tactics possibly due to their lack of interest or military knowledge, especially of the enemies of Rome. Although Cadiou is correct in regard to the sources' treatment of military issues (or lack of) many gaps can be filled, although not perfectly with the help of the findings from archaeological excavation.

It is possible to extrapolate quite a lot of information from the analysis of these findings, which in some way compensates for the deficiencies in the sources.

As for the reforms initiated by Marius, it is necessary to refer to the changes in the terms of conscription, i.e. recruitment of property-owning citizens, including those without: *capite censi* (none). Until then, recruitment of this type of citizens was done only in times of crisis, such as in the time of the Second Punic War or the Numantine war.

Keaveney explicitly argues that the reason for the reform of the conscription method employed by Marius was the shortage of soldiers for the military campaign against Jugurtha in the year 107.

It is very likely that any memories from the very long and bloody Numantine and Lusitanian wars remained fresh in the minds of the Romans by the end of the second century. The only reason why this much-needed reform was postponed was Roman conservatism.

Another innovation that is attributed to Marius is the institutionalization of the 'Marius donkey', an equipment carrier which hung from a pole, usually the shaft of a *pilum*. The carrier was developed to lessen the use of pack animals and provided a marching army with two clear advantages: a better marching speed for the legion and financial savings, a significant decrease in the number of pack animals and the food to feed them.

It seems that these carriers had been used earlier, but were not considered a standard piece of equipment for a Roman legionnaire. Metellus, predecessor to Marius as commander of the army during the Jugurthine war, used these carriers. Marius probably officially introduced the carriers to the legion, and Frontinus indicates that the 'Marius donkey' was named after him.

Marius was acquainted with Hispania during the Numantine War where he fought under the command of Scipio Aemilianus.

It is certainly possible that he learned from Aemilianus many ways to confront an 'unconventional' enemy.

Aemilianus had fought against fast and flexible enemy, against which a force the size of a legion or larger was not required. In the year 114, Marius returned to the Iberian Peninsula as the governor of Hispania Ulterior. He served in the province for two years, during which time he fought a series of battles against the local tribes. However, as there were no significant events during his tenure, on his return to Rome the Senate did not hold a victory procession in his honour.

Did the experience gained by Marius in Hispania, first as a soldier and then as a governor, serve as the catalyst for him to develop the reforms required by the Roman army?

Was the conflict against the elusive local tribes in Lusitania, who would not leave the Romans alone, the reason for the change in his perception of battle? Did his years in Hispania influence his military thinking and if so, how? Did the marches through narrow valleys of the mountains in Lusitania when attempting to locate local warriors which used guerrilla-warfare tactics, make him question the flexibility of his army?

There is no reference in the sources to these issues, and the truth is that it is hard to enter the mind of a person, to guess what he is thinking and planning in the course of a military operation. For example, were his decisions to cancel the *velites* unit in its original form and turn the *pilum* into the standard weapon for legionnaires, influenced by lessons that Marius learned during the Numantine War?

There is a direct link between the disappearance of the *velites* and the Hispanic wars. The *velites* units played an important role in battles against similar light infantry units, but failed against an enemy (Celtiberians and Lusitanias) that fought by using a wide variety of throwing weapons including *pilum*, *falcata* and others. Also, ancient sources have nothing to report, as was their habit in most matters related to changes that took place in the Roman army of the time. Archaeological findings have come to our aid in matters particularly relating to changes in military equipment and weapons, but little else.

The 200 years of fighting in Hispania played an important role in the design of the new army: the unprecedented length of military campaigns, the nature of terrain over which the wars were fought against a powerful and deceitful enemy, were among the main causes that led the Romans to transform their army and support elements in such a far-reaching way.

Chapter Six

Conclusions

The struggle by the Roman army to conquer Hispania was exacerbated by tactical and strategic problems. Local tribes fought against the Romans using various tactics, but often preferred to fight conventionally in a style similar to that of the Romans. But they also used, when required, guerrilla-warfare tactics by setting up large-scale ambushes to trap Roman forces.

According to the ancient sources, the Romans were unable to interpret correctly the 'unconventional' fighting tactics of their enemies and therefore suffered many severe defeats. The fact that the Romans treated the local tribes with disdain calling them *latrones* ('bandits') rather than warriors, led to the reality that they had not developed a military doctrine that provided a solution to guerrilla warfare. In this sense, the Hispanic Wars clearly emphasize the great importance of the leader of the Roman army. The success of eminent commanders-in-chief such as Cato or Scipio Aemilianus was exceptional.

Tactical limitations, such as supply problems or the difficult inland topography of Hispania, served as a substantial tactical advantage for the local armies while clearly holding back the Roman army. Therefore, the importance of these tactical limitations should not be underestimated. In addition, since the Roman legions were 'heavier' than Celtiberian and Lusitanian units it was harder for them to fight a 'regular' battle.

It can be concluded that the main reason for Roman military failures in their attempts to conquer Hispania, manifested by lengthy wars that lasted two centuries, were initially caused by the inferior abilities of Roman army commanders sent to that region. It is also clear that the Hispanic wars prove that the 'Advance planning theory' promoted by Harris and the 'Global strategy theory' from Lutwag do not stand the test of reality. The events in Hispania were dictated by political factors throughout the wars, and these can be divided into two.

The first factor is the discrepancy between the Republican government and the new reality of Rome becoming a superpower with vast distant territories. The second factor is that until the second half of the second century Hispania became less important to the Romans and most of their resources were diverted to the wars in the Hellenistic east.

As for the first factor, the period of the mandate granted to commanders to complete their military assignment in Hispania was suitable for wars of the fifth to third centuries but not wars of the second century. Roman army commanders in Hispania, consuls or *praetors*, did not have sufficient military forces, nor the time required to carry out their task properly to the satisfaction of the Senate and to honour Roman tradition. The short mandate was the source of many of the problems and led many army commanders to fear that they would not gain military glory or profit from their short tenure.

Therefore they initiated wars, which resulted in heavy losses to the state in both lives and money. This is added to the constant shortage of manpower which limited their ability to defeat the enemy. As a result, Roman army commanders in Hispania were forced to sign agreements with the tribe leaders. The Republican government did not have sufficient position holders available who would be capable of filling senior command positions in the army. This was a constant and very serious problem for the Roman army which spent years of continuous fighting in Hispania.

*Tabula Alcantarensis. A unconditional surrender (Deditio)
document of a tribal chief to the Roman Army, year 104.*
(Museo Arqueologico de Caceres, used with its kind permission)

The number of position holders who could constitutionally
command the army in accordance with the existing regime was
smaller than the requirements. The complex relationships between
the families controlling the Roman Senate, along with their wish
to keep hold of the reins of power, had prevented the creation of a
sufficiently wide level of senior command. These families looked for
ways to fill the growing gaps without introducing new people into
the system. These attempts did not succeed in solving the problems
and only postponed the end of the method to the first century. This is
where the second factor comes into effect. Since the importance of

Hispania was secondary to that of the Hellenistic east the same senior position holders, consuls or *praetors*, preferred to be sent to the east. But there were never sufficient to cover the many tasks.

The wars in the east against Philip V or Perseus of Macedonia or Antiochus III of the Seleucid Empire were very different from the wars against the barbarian 'gangs of bandits' in Hispania.

Rome had been forced to divert resources to Hispania in the middle of that century when the Numantine and Lusitanian wars broke out simultaneously, and especially since it had suffered serious defeats.

The Hispanic wars had undoubtedly left an indelible mark on the Roman army and it can be concluded that these wars served as the main reason for the immense transformation that the Roman army had undergone in the last century of the period of the Republic.

As described in Chapter 5, the Roman army adopted several prime weapons which originated in Hispania. The analysis of weapon collections found in the tombs of the warriors explains very clearly why the Roman army adopted these weapons. There are three important conclusions that can be drawn: the first is that at least the large Hispanic armies (Lusitanian and Celtiberian) used the frontal attack which was similar, if not identical, to that of the Romans. The second is a result of the first conclusion, the two sides used offensive weapons (for thrusting, slashing and throwing) of a similar nature and therefore it was easy for the Romans to adopt weapons used by their enemy. The third conclusion is based on material findings and the lack of reference in the sources, which make it impossible to differentiate between weapons used in 'regular' battles and those used in guerrilla fighting: apparently these were the same weapons. This, together with the lengthy duration of the wars, contributed significantly to the transformation of the Roman army into that known at the time of the *Principate*.

It can be concluded from the analysis of the sources and archaeological findings that this process of transformation, which began in the second century, gained momentum in the time of G. Marius and ended with the reforms introduced by Augustus, which transformed an army of conscripts and volunteers into a professional fighting force. This new army was made up of regular legions, and was based on cohorts rather then *manipules*. Soldiers in the legions of the new army were equipped with standard weapons provided by the State. The army commanders in distant war zones now enjoyed a wide level of autonomy and in fact, now operated independently of Rome.

There can be little doubt that the Hispanic Wars, the longest and most distant from Italy than any other war that the Romans were fighting, had a crucial impact on all of these changes.

Notes and References

1   www.principialegionis.orgfilesRoman_Army_Fo
2   It should be mentioned that Appianus was the only one who positioned Saguntum north of the river Ebro. There may be two possible explanations: the first and most likely is that Appianus was not knowledgeable of the geography of the Iberian Peninsula. The second is that he tried to defend Rome's position concerning the Saguntum affair. (*App. Hisp. 2.7.*)
3   Indicates that 8,000 of the 20,000 infantry soldiers that arrived in northern Italy with Hannibal were Iberians. (*Polyb. 3.56.4.*)
4   Livius attributes the division to the year 214. He probably got the year mixed up, as he often did, because such an early date does no seem reasonable. (*Liv. 24.41.1-42.8*)
5   Livius calls it the battle of 'Ilipa' (*Liv. 28.12*) while Appianus calls it the battle of 'Karmo'. (*Hisp. 95.26*)
6   Livius on the other hand does not specify the types of Roman forces and wrote that there had been 45,000 soldiers in total. (*Polyb. 11.20.2.*)
7   Astin claims that it is possible that Livius has received Cato's words, partial or complete, 'secondhand' through an intermediate source. In some places, Livius uses Valerius Antias and maybe even others. (*Astin, 1978. Page 307*)
8   Livius calls these tribes 'Emporitani Hispani'.
9   '...*maiores gestae res a M. Fluvio. Is apud Toletum oppidum cum Vaccaeis Vectonibusque et Celtiberis signis collatis dimicavit...*' (*Liv. 35.7,6.*)
10 Albinus won the battles 'ex-Lusitania Hispaniaque' and S. Gracchus won the battles 'ex-Celtiberis Hispaniaque'. (*Liv. 41.7.1-3.*)
11 Livius indicated that the *praetors* M. Iunius Pennus and Sempronio Lucretius were the first *praetors* whose financial benefits (*supplementa*) were revoked, due to the war effort in the east. (*Liv. 40.10.13.*)

12 Richardson has studied the relation between the size of the camp and the size of unit that inhabited it, in his article about Roman army camps in Scotland.

13 Plutarchus mentions that Caius Marius has experienced fighting a battle for the first time at the siege of Numantia. (*Plut. Mar. 3.2*)

14 Richardson's comment should be mentioned regarding the commentary in which Appianus is being interpreted. According to Richardon, Appianus' reference to the Roman Empire from the territorial aspect (*App. hisp. 99*) is contemporary (second century AD), and one cannot draw an analogy from it regarding the period on which he was writing. (*Richardson 2000, Page 178*)

15 Orosius was wrong in writing that the war had started in the year 28; Augustus could not have gone out on a war prior to receiving his *imperium* in 27. (*Orosius 6.21*)

16 According to Suetonius, Augustus fell of his horse while crossing a bridge that had collapsed, and so he broke his leg and two arms. On the other hand, Dio Cassius wrote that Augustus has become ill due to physical and psychological overload.

17 '*Signa militaria complura per alios duces amissa devictis hostibus reciperavi ex Hispania ...*' (*Aug. R.G. 29*)

18 Two of them were 'new people' who were supported by noble patron-friends; Cato used the help of Valerius Flaccus in 195, and Glabrio received the consulate with the help of the Scipios in 191. (*Scullard, 1980. Page 332*)

19 Rich & Shipley, 1993.

20 We should point out here that according to Harmand, many researchers overestimate the importance of the plundering and booty as motives of the Roman leaders. (*Harmand 1967, Page 411*)

21 ...'*bellum se ipsum alet*'... (*Liv. 34.9.12*)

22 Roth claims that it was groups of *contubernium* (eight soldiers). (*Roth, 1998. Page 330*)

23 Livius uses the word *cogebat*, which emphasizes the obligation of each soldier. (*Liv. 26.8.9*)

24 Livius calls these kings '*latrones latronumque duces*' (thief leaders or thugs). (*Liv. 28.32.9*)

25 'Only iron' in Latin.

26 The same event appears with slight differences also in Polybius' works (*Polyb. 10.19*): Livius (*Liv. 26.50. 1-12*): Valerius Maximus. (*Val. Max. 4.3.1*)

27 It is interesting to point out that Shulten links this event to the solar eclipse that took place on 1 April 136 (*Shulten, 1957. Page 365*).

28 '*... cum pares bello aequo foedere in pacem...veniret.*' (*Liv. 34. 57, 7-9*)

29 '(Viriathus) had the best leadership capabilities among the barbarians... the most daring ... Always in front of everyone ... in eight years of war, his army which was made of different elements never revolted against him (and the army) has always obeyed his instructions and was willing to confront danger'. (*App. Hisp. 75*)

30 Appianus also mentioned this battle, but he wrote in general and did not detail the size of the different forces. (*App. Hisp. 25-28*)

31 '*ut emissis soliferreis falaricisque gladios strinxerunt..*' (*Liv. 34.14, 10*)

32 The battle of Saltus Manlianus. (*Liv. 40.40*)

33 '*ubi ordinata acie et signis collatis se non esse pares legionibus senserunt, cuneo impresionem fecerunt.*'(*Liv. 40.40*)

34 '*prima luce ad sextam horam diei signis collatis pugnasse, multos utrimque cecidisse.*' (*Liv. 40.50*)

35 '*Desilite, inquit, milites, nisi vultis aquilam hostibus prodere: ego certe meum rei publicae atque imperatori officium praestitero.*' (*Caes. Gal. 4.25*)

36 '*... sed intolerantius Gallos insequentes legio... decima tardavit, quae pro subsidio paulo aequiore loco constiterat ... Verkingetorix ad radicibus collis suos intra.*'

Bibliography

Texts and Translations

Ammianus Marcellinus: *Res Gestae*, Translated by J.C. Rolfe, London, 1948.

Appianus: *Appian's Roman History: The Wars in Spain*, Translated by H. White, Harvard, 1972.

Augustus: *Res Gestae Divi Augusti* (*The Acts of Augustus*), Translated by W. Shipley, London, 1979.

Cicero: *De Officiis*, Translated by W.G. Williams, London, 1954.

Cicero: *De Legibus*, Translated by K. Clinton Walker, London, 1928.

Dio Cassius: *Roman History*, Translated by E. Carey, London, 1927.

Diodorus Siculus: *The Library of History*, Translated by C.H. Oldfather, London, 1933.

Frontinus: *The Stratagematon*, Edited by M.B. Mc Elwain, London, 1950.

Herodotos: *The Histories*, Translated by A.D. Godley, London, 1925.

Iosephus Flavius: De Bello Iudaico, Translated by J.M. Cordero, Buenos Aires, 1943.

Iulius Caesar: *De Bello Civico*, Translated by A.G. Peskett, London, 1914.

Idem: *De Bello Gallico*, Translated by A.G. Peskett, London, 1914.

Idem: *De Bello Alexandrino*, *De Bello Africo*, *De Bello Hispaniensi*, Translated by A.G. Way, London, 1955.

Livius: *Ab Urbe Condita*, Translated by Evan T. Stage, London, 1935.

Lucius Annaeus Florus: *Epitomae De Tito Livio Bellorum Omnium Anorvm DCC*, Libri II, Translated by W. Heinemann, London, 1928.

Orosius Paulus: *Historiarum Adversum Paganos*, Translated by Olms. G, Hildesheim, 1967

Plinius Maior: *Naturalis Historia*, Translated by H. Rackham, London, 1928.

Plinius Minor: *Epistulae*, Translated by B. Radice, Harvard, 1969.

Plutarchus: *Lives: Augustus*, Translated by B. Perrin, London, 1914.

Idem: *Lives: Caius Marius*, Translated by B. Perrin, Harvard, 1950

Idem: Lives: Marcus Cato, Translated by B. Perrin, Harvard, 1959

Idem: *Lives: Sertorius*, Translated by B. Perrin, London, 1914.

Idem: *Lives: The Gracchi*, Translated by B. Perrin, London, 1914.

Idem: *Moralia*, Translated by W. Heinemann, London, 1927.

Polybius: *The Histories*, Translated by W. Heinemann, London, 1922.

Seneca: *De Beneficiis*, Translated by J.W. Basore, London, 1928

Silius *Italicus: Punica*, Translated by J.D. Duff, London, 1934.

Strabo: *The Geography*, Translated by L. Jones London 1966.

Sallustius: *Bellum Iugurthinum*, Translated by S. A. Handford, Middlesex, 1963.

Suetonius: *De Vita Caesarum*, Translated by J. C. Rolfe, London, 1979.

Tacitus: *Annals*, Translated by J. Jackson, Harvard, 1979.

Thucydides: *The Peloponnesian War*, Translated by J.H. Finley, Harvard, 1962.

Valerius Maximus: *Factorum et Ictorum Memorabilivm, Libri Novem*, Translated by Y. Fromion, Paris, 1864.

Velleius Paterculus: *Historiae Romanae*, Translated by W. Shipley, London 1979.

Vegetius: *Epitomae (of Military Science)*, Translated by N.P. Miller, Liverpool, 1975.

General Works

Adcock, F.E: T*he Roman Art of War under the Republic*, Cambridge, 1960.

Alarcão, J: *Novas perspectivas sobre os Lusitanos*, RPA Vol 4, No. 2, Lisbon, 2001.

Alarcão, J: *Roman Portugal*, Warminster, 1988.

Almagro Gorbea, A: *Hispania a la llegada de Roma*, 1998.

Alston, R: *Roman Military Pay from Caesar to Diocletian*, JRS 84, pages 113-123, 1994

Alvar, J: *La jefatura como instrumento de análisis para el historiador: basileia griega y régulos ibéricos*, in Espacio y Organización Social, Madrid, 1990.

Álvarez, R. and Cubero, M: *Los Pila del Poblado Ibérico de Castellruf.* Gladius XIX, pages 120-142, Madrid, 1999.

Álvarez Sanchíz, J.R: *Los Vettones*, Madrid, 1999.

Andreotti, C. C: La Construcción de los espacios políticos Ibéricos entre los siglos III y I A.C.: *Algunas cuestiones metodológicas e históricas a partir de Polibio y Estrabon*, CuPUAM, 28-29, pages. 35-54, 2002-2003.

Arnold, W.T: *The Roman System of Provincial Administration to the Accession of Constantine the Great*, Oxford, 1990.

Arrayás Morales, I: Tarraco: *Capital Provincial,* Gerión 22 (1), pages 291-303, 2004.

Astin, A.E: *The Roman Commander in Hispania Ulterior in 142 BC*, Historia 13, pages 245-254, 1964.

Astin, A.E: *Scipio Aemilianus*, Oxford, 1967.

Astin, A.E: *Foreign Policy Dictated by Structure of Government and Character of Generals* in Gruen, E.S: *Imperialism in the Roman Republic*, pages 66-71, 1970.

Astin, E.A: *Cato the Censor*, Oxford, 1978.

Aurrecoechea, J. *Roman Military Equipment in Spain*, in Morillo, A and Aurrecoechea, J: *The Roman Army in Hispania*, Leon, 2006.

Austin, N.J.E and Rankov, B: *Exploratio: Military and Political Intelligence in the Roman World from the Second Punic War to the Battle of Adrianople*, New York, 1995.

Azov, A: *Reconnaissance and Intelligence Units in the Roman Army – Exploratores: from Julius Caesar to the Third Century AD*, Tel Aviv, (in Hebrew), 1993.

Badian, E: *Foreign Clientelae (264-70 BC)*, Oxford, 1958.

Badian, E: *Roman Imperialism in the late Republic*, Oxford, 1968.

Balbuena, M.Y and, Munian, J: *Julio Cesar, Comentarios*, Barcelona, 1962.

Beard, M. and Crawford, M: *Rome in the Late Republic: Problems of Interpretation*, London, 1985.

Bell, M.J.V: *Tactical Reform in the Roman Republican Army*. HISTORIA 14, pages 404-422, 1965.

Bernstein, A.H: *Tiberius Sempronius Gracchus: Tradition and Apostasy*, Cornell, 1978.

Berrocal-Rangel, L: *Aproximaciónes a la demografía de la Celtiberia, Entre Celtas e Íberos*, pages 89-106. Madrid, 2001.

Berrocal-Rangel, L: *Episodios de guerra en los poblados indígenas de Hispania celtica: criterios para la identificación arqueológica de la conquista romana.* Saldvie 8, pages 181-191, Madrid, 2008.

Billows, R: *International Relations*, in The Cambridge History of Greek and Roman Warfare, Vol. 1, pages 303-324, Cambridge, 2008.

Birley, A. R: Hadrian: The Restless Emperor, London and New York, 1997.

Bishop, M. C: *The Production and Distribution of Roman Military Equipment*, BAR, pages 2-12, Oxford, 1985.

Bishop, M. C: *Roman Military Equipment*, Latomus 58, 1998.

Bishop, M.C and Coulston, J.C.N: *Roman Military Equipment: From the Punic Wars to the fall of Rome*, London, 1993.

Bishop, M.C: *O Fortuna: a sideways look at the Archaeological Record and Roman Military Equipment*. BAR, Oxford, 1989.

Blazquez, J.M: *Campamentos Romanos en la Meseta Hispana en la época Romano-Republicana, in Celtiberia*, Zaragoza, 1996.

Blazquez, J.M: *El Estado Burebista y los pueblos de la Península Ibérica en época helenística*, Geríon 5, Universidad Compluetense de Madrid, 1987.

Blazquez, J.M: *El impacto de la conquista de Hispania en Roma*, Klio 41, pages 167-186, 1963.

Blazquez, J.M: *España Romana*, Madrid, 1996.

Blazquez, J.M: *La Romanización. en Sobre los graves problemas economicos y sociales de los celtibéricos y lusitanos*, pages 191-215, Madrid, 1974.

Borja, D. A: *Un quaestor pro praetore republicano en Carthago Nova*, JRS Vol 21, pages 255-266, 2008.

Bosch, P.G: *España Romana* (218 a. de JC- 414 de JC), Madrid, 1955.

Bowersock, G: *Augustus and the East: The Problem of Succession*, in Millar, F. and Segal, E: *Caesar Augustus – Seven Aspects*, pages 168-188, Oxford, 1984.

Bowersock, G: *Augustus and the Greek World*, Oxford, 1966.

Breeze, D: *Why did the Romans fail to conquer Scotland?* ProcSocAntiqScot 118, pages 3-22, 1988.

Brizzi, G: *I sistemi informativi dei Romani: principi e realtà nell'età delle conquiste Oltremare* (218 - 168 BC), Wiesbaden, 1982.

Broughton, T.S.R: *Magistrates of the Roman Republica*, pages 143-135, New York, 1986.

Brunt, P.A: *Italian Manpower 225 BC to 14 AD*, Oxford, 1971.

Brunt, P.A: *The Army and the Land in the Roman Revolution*, JRS 52, pages 69-86, 1962.

Buchan, J: *Julius Caesar*, Edinburgh, 1932.

Buchan, J: *Augustus*, Cambridge, 1937.

Buril Lo Mozota, F: *La ciudad celtibérica de Segeda 1. Nuevos hallazgos*, Zaragoza, 2001

Burns, M. T: *The Homogenization of Military Equipment under the Roman Republic*, Digressus Supplement 1, pages 60-85, London, 2003.

Cadiou, F : *Hiberia in terra miles: les armées romaines et la conquête de l'Hispania sous la République* (218-45 av. JC). Madrid. 2007

Cadiou, F : *Les guerres en Hispania et l'émergence de la cohorte légionnaire dans l'armée romaine sous la République: une révision critique*. Gladius XXI, pages 167-182, 2001.

Campbell, B: *Greek and Roman Military Writers; Selected Readings*, London, 2004.

Campbell, B: *War and Society in Imperial Rome 31 BC-AD 284*, London, 2002.

Carrasco Serrano, G: *La Presencia Romana en Castilla-La Mancha: La Anexión del Territorio*. Revista De Estudios Albacetenses, No. 47, pages 41-56, Albacete, 2003.

Carretero, V.S: *El Ejercito Romano Del Noroeste Peninsular Durante El Alto Imperio*. Gladius XIX, pages 47-70, 2000.

Carretero, V.S: *Hacia La Definición De Un Nuevo Grupo Vascular Del Noroeste Hispanico En Época Romana*. BSAA LXVI, pages 127-149, 2000.

Carter, M. J: *Buttons and Wooden Swords: Polybius 10.20.3, Livy 26.51 and the Rudis*. Cl. Phil 101, pages 153-160, Chicago, 2006.

Castren, P: *About the Legio X Equestris*. Arctos 8, pages 5-7, 1974.

Cerdan, A.M: *Campamentos romanos en España a través de los textos clásicos*. Hist. Ant. t 6, pages 379-398, 1993.

Cerdan, A.M: *The Roman Army and Urban Development in N.W. Spain Asturica Augusta and Legio VII Gemina*, Madrid, 2006.

Cerdeño, M.L with Sagardoy, T and Chorda, M: *Fortificaciones celtibéricas frente a Roma: El oppidum de Los Rodiles*, Complutum Vol 19, pages 173-189, 2008.

Chapman, C.E: *A History of Spain*, New York, 1965.

Clavell, J: *Sun Tzu: The Art of War*, New York, 1988.

Connolly, P: *Pilum, Gladius, and Pugio in the Late Republic*. JRES 8, pages 41-57, 1997.

Connolly, P: *The Greek Armies*, London, 1978.

Connolly, P: *The Pilum from Marius to Nero – a Consideration of its Development and Function*. JRES 12-13, Oxford, 2001-2002.

Connolly, P: *The Roman Fighting Technique deduced from Armour and Weaponry*. Roman Frontier Studies, pages 358-366, 1989.

Corzo Sánchez: *La Segunda Guerra Púnica en Baetica*. Habis 6, pages 213-240, 1975.

Crawford, M. H: *Roman Republican Coinage*, Cambridge, 1974.

Crawford, M. H: *The Roman Republic*, London, 1993.

Curchin, L. A: *Roman Spain, Conquest and Assimilation*, New York, 1991.

Curchin, L. A: *The Romanization of Central Spain: Complexity, Diversity, and Change in a Provincial Hinterland*, London, 2004.

Dando-Collins, S: *Caesar's Legion*, New Jersey, 2002.

Davies, G: *Roman Siege Works*, Gloucester, 2006.

Davies, R: *Service in the Roman Army*, Edinburgh, 1989.

Dawson, D: *The Origins of Western Warfare*, New York, 1996.

De Arriba, G: *Cerámicas Griegas de la Península Ibérica*, Valencia, 1967.

De Souza, P: *Naval Battle and Siege*. The Cambridge History of Greek and Roman Warfare Vol. 1, pages 435- 460, Cambridge, 2008.

De Souza, P: *Piracy in the Graeco-Roman World*, Cambridge, 2002.

Dixon, R.K and Southern, P: *The Roman Cavalry*, London, 1997.

Dorey, T. A and Dudley, D. R: *Rome and Carthage*, London, 1971.

Dyson, S. L: *Native Revolts in the Roman Empire*. Historia 20, pages 239-274, 1971.

Erdkamp, P: *War and State Formation in the Roman Republic. A Companion to the Roman Army*, pages 96-113, Oxford, 2008.

Espelosin, F: *La Imagen del Bárbaro en Apiano - La Adaptabilidad de un Modelo Retorico*. Habis 24, pages 105-124, 1993.

Fabião, C: *The Roman Army in Portugal*, in: Morillo, A and Aurrecoechea, J: *The Roman Army in Hispania*, Leon, 2006.

Fabricus, E: *Some Notes on Polybius' Description of Roman Camps*, in: Miller, M.C.J and De Voto, J.G: *Polybius and Pseudo-Hyginus: The Fortification of the Roman Camp*, pages 45-44, Chicago, 1994.

Fear, E.T: *The Vernacular Legion of Hispania Ulterior*. Latomus 50, pages 809-821, 1991.

Fernández Ibañez, C: *Metalistería militar romana en el norte de la Península Ibérica durante los periodos republicano y alto imperial*. BAR 1371, pages 183-208, Oxford, 2005.

Fernández Riel, P: *Fases de la conquista romana e inico del asentamiento*, in Pizarro Moreno, M: *Hispania: El legado de Roma*, pages 51-64, Zaragoza, 1998.

Fernandez, E: *Escénas de la guerra contra Sertorio*, Madrid, 2000.

Fernandez, P.U. *The Roman Conquest and Organization of the Iberian Peninsula*, in Morillo, A and Aurrecoechea, J: *The Roman Army in Hispania*, Leon, 2006.

Ferrero, G: *The Life of Caesar*, London, 1933.

Feugère, M: *Weapons of the Romans*, Tempus, 2002.

Fiorato, V: *The Archaeology of a Mass Grave from the Battle of Towton, AD 1461*, Oxford, 2000.

Foss, C: *Roman Historical Coins*, London, 1990.

Frank, T: *An Economic History of Rome*, New York, 1962.

Frank, T: *Reaction to Spanish Treachery*, in Gruen E.S: *Imperialism in the Roman Republic*, pages 57-60, 1970.

Frank, T: *The Roman Imperialism*, New York, 1929.

Gabba, E: *Republican Rome: The Army and the Allies*, Berkeley, 1976.

Gann, L.H: *Guerrillas in History*, Stanford, 1971.

Garcia Riaza, E: *La funcion de los rehenes en la diplomacia Hispano Republicana*. MemHistAnt XVIII, pages 81-107, 2008.

García y Bellido, A: *Álbum de dibujos de la colección de bronces antiguos de Antonio Vives Escudero*. AEspA. XIII, Madrid, 1993.

García y Bellido, A: *Fenicios y Cartaginenses en occidente*, Madrid, 1942.

García y Bellido, A: *Hispani tumultantes: de Numancia a Sertorio*, Alcalá de Henares, Madrid, 1987.

Garlan, Y: *War In The Ancient World*, New York, 1975.

Garlan, Y: *War in the Ancient World: A Social History*, New York, 1975.

Garzetti, A: *Caesar*, Oxford, 1968.

Garzetti, A: *From Tiberius to the Antonines*, London, 1974.

Garzetti, A: *The Roman Nobility*, Oxford, 1969.

Gilliam, B.F: *Roman Army Papers*, Amsterdam, 1986.

Gilliver, C: *Battle; The Cambridge History of Greek and Roman Warfare*, Vol. II, pages 122-157, 2007.

Gilliver, C: *The Roman Art of War*, London, 1998.

Gimeno Pascual, H: *El descubrimiento de Hispania, in Pizarro Moreno*, M: Hispania: *El legado de Roma*, pages 25-36, Zaragoza, 1998.

Goldsworthy, A. K: *The Roman Army at War*, Oxford, 1998.

Goldsworthy, A. K: War; *The Cambridge History of Greek and Roman Warfare*, Vol. II, pages 76-121, 2007.

Gomez-Pantoja, J: *Pecora consectari: transhumance in Roman Spain*, in Frizell B.S: *Man and Animal in Antiquity*, pages 94-102, Rome, 2004.

Gonzales, E.C: *Viriato y el ataque a la ciudad de Segobriga*, RPA Vol 10, pages 239-246, 2007.

Griffin, M: *The 'Fall' of the Scipios*, in Malkin, I and., Rubinshon Z.W: *Leaders and Masses in the Roman World*, Leiden, 1995.

Grimal, P: *Le siècle des Scipions*, Paris, 1975.

Greenlees Zollschan, L: *Roman Diplomacy and the Jewish Embassy of 161 BCE*, Beer Sheva, (in Hebrew), 2005.

Gruen E. S: *Imperialism in the Roman Republic*, Berkeley, 1970.

Gruen E. S: *Roman Politics and the Criminal Courts, 149-78 BC*, Cambridge, 1968.

Gruen E. S: *The Imperial Policy of Augustus*, in Raaflaub, K and Toher, M: *Between Republic and Empire*, pages 395-416, Berkeley, 2001.

Harmand, J : *L'armée et le soldat à Rome, de 107 à 50 avant notre ère*; Paris, 1967.

Harris, R.J: *Spain at the Dawn of History*, London, 1998.

Harris, W.V: *War and Imperialism in Republican Rome 327-70 BC*, Oxford, 1979.

Hidalgo, M.J: *Ancient History in Spanish Historiography*, Salamanca, 2000.

Holder, P.A: *The Auxilia from Augustus to Hadrian*, London, 1980.

Hölscher, T: *Images of War in Greece and Rome: Between Military Practice, Public Memory, and Cultural Symbolism*, JRS, pages 1-17, 2005.

Howgego, I: *The Supply and Use of Money in the Roman World 200 BC to AD 300*, JRS LXXXII, pages 1-32, 1992.

Hoyos, D: *The Age of Overseas Expansion (264-146 BC), A Companion to the Roman Army*, pages 63-79, Oxford, 2008.

Hurtado Aguna, J: *La Presencia del Ejercito Romano en Carpetania*, MemHistAnt XXI-XXII, pages 73-86, 2000.

Kaldor, M: *New & Old Wars*, Cambridge, 1999.

Keaveney, A: *The Army at the Roman Revolution*, New York, 2007.

Keay, S.J: *Roman Spain*, London, 1988.

Keppie, L: 1998. *The Making of the Roman Army: From Republic to Empire*, London.

Klein, S; Rico, C and Brey, G.P: *Copper Ingots from the Western Mediterranean Sea*, JRS, Vol 20, pages 203-222, 2007.

Knapp, R.C: *Aspects of the Roman Experience in Iberia 206-100 BC*, Valladolid, 1977.

Knapp, R.C: *Roman provinces of Iberia to 100 BC*, Michigan, 1973.

Konrad, C.F: *Commentary on Plutarch's Life of Sertorius*, Michigan, 1986.

Laqueur, W: *Guerrilla*, London, 1977.

Lazenby, J.F: *Hannibal's War*, Warminster, 1978.

Le Bohec, Y : *César Chef de Guerre*, Paris, 2001.

Le Bohec, Y : *Histoire militaire des guerres puniques*, Monaco, 1996.

Le Bohec, Y : *L'armement des romains pendant les guerres puniques d'après les sources littéraires*, JRES 8, pages 13-24, 1997.

Le Bohec, Y : *Les légions de Rome sous le Haut-Empire*, Lyon, 2000.

Le Bohec, Y: *The Imperial Roman Army*, New York, 1994.

Lendon, J.E: *Soldiers & Ghosts*, London, 2005.

Livermore, H. V: *The Origins of Spain and Portugal*, London, 1971.

Lorrio, A.J: *Los Celtibericos*, Alicante, 1997.

Lorrio, A.J: *Los Celtíberos: análisis arqueológico de un proceso de etnogenesis*, Revista de Guimarães, Special Volume I, pages 297-319, Guimarães, 1999.

Luttwak, E.N: *The Grand Strategy of The Roman Empire*, London, 1993.

Madden, F. W: *A Dictionary of Roman Coins*, Hildesheim, 1969.

Maggie, P: *Augustus' War in Spain*, Cl. Phil. 15, pages 322-342, 1920.

Mann, J. C: *The Raising of New legions during the Principate*, Hermes 91, pages 483-489, 1998.

Martin, J.M: *Conquista y romanización de Lusitania*, Salamanca, 1988.

McCall, J.B: *The Cavalry of the Roman Republic*, London, 2002.

Mierse, W: *Augustan Building Programs in the Western Provinces*, in *Between Republic and Empire*, pages 308-333, Berkeley, 1990.

Millan, L. J: *La batalla de Ilipa*, Habis 17, pages 283-303, 1986.

Millar, F: *Emperors, Frontiers and Foreign Relations, 31 BC-AD 378*, Britannia 13, pages 1-23, 1982.

Millar, F: *The Roman Empire and its Neighbours*, London, 1967.

Miller, M. C. J and De Voto, J. G: *Polybius and Pseudo-Hyginus: The Fortification of the Roman Camp*, Chicago, 1994.

Molina Vidal, J: *Vinculaciones entre Apulia y el area de influencia de Cartago Nova en época tardorrepublicana*, Latomus Vol 58, pages 6-27, 1999.

Mommsen, T: *The History of Rome*, New York, 1903.

Mommsen, T: *The Provinces of the Roman Empire*, London, 1968.

Monet, P and Quesada, F: *La Guerra en el Mundo Celtibérico* (ss.VI-II a. de C), Madrid, 2002.

Mora, G: *Roman Military Archaeology in Spain: A History of Research*, in: Morillo, A. and Aurrecoechea, J: *The Roman Army in Hispania*, Leon, 2006.

Morales, H.F: *Why la Rasa was not a Camp of the Scipionic Siege of Numantia*, Madrid, 2005.

Moret, P. *Los monarcas ibéricos en Polibio y Tito Livio*. CuPUAM 28-29, pages 23-33, Madrid, 2003.

Morillo, A and Aurrecoechea J: *The Roman Army in Hispania*, Leon, 2006.

Morillo, A and Hernández E.M: E*l Ejercito Romano en la Península Ibérica, De la Arqueología Filológica a la Arqueología Militar Romana*,

Estudios Humanísticos, Historia 4, pages 177-207, Leon, 2005.

Morillo, A: *La 'Legio III Macedonica' en la peninsula: el campamento de Herrera de Pisuerga (Palencia)*, Madrid, 2005.

Morillo, A: *Legio VII Gemina and its Flavian Fortress*, Leon, 2004.

Morillo, A: *Roman military productions in Spain*, in Morillo, A and Aurrecoechea, J: *The Roman Army in Hispania*, Leon, 2006.

Morillo, A: *The Roman Army in Spain*, in: Morillo, A and Aurrecoechea, J: T*he Roman Army in Hispania*, Leon, 2006.

Nilsson, M.P: *The Introduction of Hoplite Tactics at Rome*, JRS, Vol 19, pages 1-11, 1929.

Nuñez, E and Quesada S.F: *Una Sepultura con Armas de Baja Época Ibérica en la Necrópolis Del Cerro De Las Balas*, Gladius XX, pages 91-219, 2000.

Palencia F.J.S and Orejas, A: *Minería en la Hispania romana; Hispania: El legado de Roma,* pages 103-112, Zaragoza, 1998.

Parker, H.M.D: *The Roman Legions*, New York, 1971.

Patterson, J: *Military Organization and Social Change in Later Roman Republic*, London, 1980.

Patterson, J: *Military Organization and Social Change in the Later Roman Republic; War and society in the Roman World*, pages 92-112, London, 1993.

Peddie, J: *The Roman War Machine*, Gloucestershire, 1995.

Perez, A.A: *Problemática en torno al estudio de la figura de Viriato*, Panta Rei I, pages 45-60, Madrid, 2006.

Pina Polo, F: *El Oppidum Castra Aelia y las campañas de Sertorius en los años 77-76 ac*, JRA 11, pages 245-264, 1998.

Pizarro Moreno, M: *Hispania*, pages 37-50, Zaragoza, 2004.

Pizarro Moreno, M: *Hispania: El legado de Roma*, Zaragoza, 1998.

Potter, D: *The Roman Army and Navy*, in: Harriet I.F: *The Cambridge Companion to The Roman Republic*, pages 41-59, Cambridge, 2004.

Quesada, S.F: *'La Arqueología de los campos de batalla'*, Notas para un estado de la questión y una guía de investigación, Madrid, 2008.

Quesada, S.F: *En torno al análisis táctico de las fortificaciones ibéricas, Algunos puntos de vista alternativos*, Gladius XXI, pages 145-154, 2001.

Quesada, S.F: *Gladius Hispaniensis: an Archaeological View from Iberia*, JRES Vol 8, pages 251-270, 1997.

Quesada, S.F: *Hispania y el ejercito Romano Republicano, Interacción y adopción de tipos metálicos*, Santander, 2007.

Quesada, S.F: *Innovaciones de raíz helenística en el armamento y tácticas de los pueblos Ibéricos desde el siglo III ac*, CuPAUAM 28-29, pages 69-94, 2003.

Quesada, S.F: *Los Celtibéricos y la guerra: tácticas, cuerpos, efectivos y bajas, in Burillo, F: Segeda y su contexto histórico*, pages 149-177, Madrid, 2006.

Quesada, S.F: *Not so different: individual fighting techniques and battle tactics of Roman and Iberian armies within the framework of warfare in the Hellenistic Age*, Pallas 70, pages 245-263, 2006.

Rankin, D: *Celts and the Classical World*, London, 1996.

Rankov, B: *Military Forces, The Cambridge History of Greek and Roman Warfare*, Vol 2, pages 30-75, Cambridge, 2007.

Rich, J and Shipley, R.J: *War and Society in the Roman World*, London, 1993.

Rich, J.W: *Declaring War in the Roman Republic in the Period of Transmarine Expansion*, Brussels, 1976.

Richardson, J.S: *Appians' Wars of the Romans in Iberia*, Warminster, 2000.

Richardson, J.S: *Hispaniae: Spain and the Development of Roman Imperialism, 218-82 BC*, Cambridge. 1986.

Richardson, J.S: *Roman Provincial Administration, 227 BC to AD 117*, Bristol, 1984.

Richardson, J.S: *The Order of Battle in the Roman Army: Evidence from Marching Camps*, OxFJA, Oxford, 2001.

Roda De Lanza, I: *The Cantabrian Wars and the reorganization of the Iberian Peninsula*; in Morillo, A and Aurrecoechea, J: *The Roman Army in Hispania*, Leon, 2006.

Rodriguez Colmenero, A: *Augusto e Hispania: Conquista y organización de Norte Peninsular*, Bilbao, 1979.

Rodriguez, R: *Baetica and Germania. Notes on the Concept of 'Provincial Interdependence' in the Roman Empire*; in Erdkamp, P: *The Roman*

Army and the Economy, pages 12-29, Amsterdam, 2002.

Roldan Hervas, J: *El ejercito romano en Hispania*; in Pizarro Moreno, M: Hispania: *El legado de Roma*, pages 65-73, Zaragoza, 1998.

Rostovtzeff, M: *Rome*, Oxford, 1960.

Rostovtzeff, M: *Vexillum and victory*, JRS 32, pages 92-106, Oxford, 1942.

Roth, J.P: *The Logistics of The Roman Army at war, 265 BC-AD 235*, Brill, 1998.

Roxan, M. M: *The Auxilia of the Roman Army raised in the Iberian Peninsula*, London, 1973.

Ruiz, A and Molinos, M: *The Archaeology of the Iberians*, Cambridge, 1998.

Sabben-Clare, J: *Caesar and Roman Politics*, Oxford, 1971.

Sabin, P: Battle, *The Cambridge History of Greek and Roman Warfare*, Vol 1, pages 399-435, Cambridge, 2008.

Sabin, P: *The face of roman battle*, JRS 90, pages 1-17, 2000.

Saez Abad, R: *La maquinaria bélica en Hispania, Crónica de un siglo de investigaciones*, Murcia, 2005.

Salinas de Frias, M: *Conquista y romanización de Celtiberia*, Salamanca, 1996.

Salinas de Frias, M: *La jefatura de Viriato y las sociedades del occidente de la Península Ibérica*, Paleohispánica 8, pages 89-120, 2008.

Sanchez Moreno, E: *Algunas notas sobre la guerra como estrategia de interacción social en la Hispania prerromana: Viriato, jefe redistributivo*, Habis 33, pages 141-174, 2002.

Santos Yanguas, N. *Los recintos fortificados como marco del desarrollo de la cultura castrenia en el norte de la península ibérica*, Espacio, Tiempo y Forma. Serie II, pages 437-467, Oviedo, 2007.

Santos Yanguas, N: *Astures y Cántabros: Estudio etno-geográfico*, Espacio Tiempo y Forma, Serie II, pages 418-436, Oviedo, 2006.

Santos Yanguas, N: *El ejército y la romanización de Galicia: conquista y anexión del noroeste de la Península Ibérica*, Oviedo, 1988.

Schulten, A: *Iberische Landeskunde*, Strasburg, 1957.

Schulten, A: *Las fuentes desde el 500 antes de JC hasta Caesar*, Fontes

Hispaniae Antiquae II, Barcelona, 1925.

Schulten, A: *Numantia I-IV*, Munich, 1929.

Schulten, A: *Pilum*, in Pauly-Wissowa, R.E: pages 1333-1370, Stuttgart, 1943.

Schulten, A: *Sertorius*, New York, 1975.

Scullard, H. H: *A History of the Roman World from 146 to 30 BC*, London, 1963.

Scullard, H. H: *A History of the Roman World from 753 to 146 BC*, London, 1980.

Scullard, H. H: *A Note on the Battle of Ilipa*, JRS 26, pages 19-24, 1936.

Scullard, H. H: *From the Gracchi to Nero*, New York, 1959.

Scullard, H. H: *Scipio Aemilianus and Roman Politics*, JRS 50, pages 59-74, 1960.

Scullard, H. H: *Scipio Africanus in the Second Punic War*, Cambridge, 1930.

Scullard, H. H: *Scipio Africanus: Soldier and Politician*, Thames & Hudson, 1970.

Segui Marco, J. J: *La Historia Militar del Levante español en la Edad Antigua*, Militaría, No. 11, pages 17-33, Madrid, 1998.

Serrão, J: *Diccionario de Historia de Portugal*, Porto, 1984.

Sherwin-White, A.N: *Roman Foreign Policy in the East 168 BC to AD 14*, University of Oklahoma Press, 1973.

Sidebottom, H: *International Relations*, The Cambridge History of Greek and Roman Warfare, Vol II, pages 3-29, Cambridge, 2007.

Simkins, M: *The Roman Army from Caesar to Trajan*, London, 1984.

Shatzman, I: *The History of the Roman Republic*, (in Hebrew), Jerusalem, 1989.

Smith, R.E: *Service in the Post-Marian Army*, Manchester, 1958.

Smith, W. A: *Dictionary of Greek and Roman Geography*, New York, 1966.

Soldevilla, F and Taberner, F: *Historia de Catalunya*, Madrid, 1982.

Soldevilla, F: *Historia de España*, Barcelona, 1961.

Sopenia, G: *Celtiberian Ideologies and Religion*, Journal of Interdisciplinary Celtic Studies, Vol 6, pages 347-410, 2005. (ISSN 1540-4889 online)

Southern, P: *Augustus*, New York, 1998.

Southern, P: *The Roman Army*, Oxford, 2007.

Spaul, J: *Cohorts: The History and a Short List*, Bar 841, Oxford, 2000.

Speidel, M.P: *Roman Army Studies*, Vol 2, University of Hawaii, 1982.

Stylow, A.U: *Los Inicios de la Epigrafía Latina en la Baetica, El Ejemplo de la Epigrafía Funeraria*; Roma y el Nacimiento de la Cultura Epigráfica en España, pages 219-245, Madrid, 1995.

Sumner, G.V: *Proconsuls and Provinciae in Spain 218/7-196/5 BC*, Arethusa 3, pages 85-102, 1970.

Sumner, G.V: *The Legion and the Centuriate Organization*, JRS Vol. 60, pages 67-78, 1970.

Syme, R: *The Spanish War of Augustus*, American Journal of Philology 54, pages 293-317, 1934.

Syme, R: *The Conquest of the North West Spain, Legio VII Gemina*, American Joournal of Philology 91, pages 83-107, 1970.

Talbert, R.J.A: *Atlas of Classical History*, London, 1985.

Torradel, M: *Iberian Art*, New York, 1978.

Torregaray Pagola, E: *Memoria como instrumento en Historia Antigua. La transmisión de la memoria de los Cornelii Scipiones*, Latomus Vol 61, pages 295-311, 2002.

Trevino, R: *Rome's Enemies 4; Spanish Armies*, London, 1992.

Trevino, R: *Spanish Armies 218 BC-19 BC*, London, 1996.

Troncoso, V.A: *Primeras etapas en la conquista romana de Gallaecia*, Militaría 8, pages 53-68, UCM, Madrid, 1996.

Ulbert, G: *Cáceres el Viejo*, MB 11, Mainz am Rhein, 1984.

Van Gennep, A: *The Rites of Passage*, Chicago, 1960.

Velaza Frias, J: *Nuevos testimonios de la guerra sertoriana en Calahorra: Un deposito de proyectiles de catapulta*, Kalakorikos 8, La Rioja, 2003.

Vives, J: *Inscripciones Latinas de la España Romana: Antología de 6800 textos*, Barcelona, 1971-1972.

Walbank, F.W: *A Historical commentary on Polybiu*s, Oxford, 1957.

Warry, J: *Warfare in the Classical World*, Dallas, 2001.

Watson, G.R: *The Roman Soldier*, Bristol, 1961.

Webster, G: *The Roman Imperial Army of the First and Second Centuries AD*, London, 1969.

Wheeler, E.L: *Firepower: Missile Weapons and the 'Face of Battle'*, JRMS 5, pages 169-183, 2001.

Willkes, J: *The Roman Army*, Cambridge, 1972.

Wiseman, T.P: *New Men in the Roman Senate 139 BC-AD 14*, Oxford, 1971.

Yavetz, Z: *Julius Caesar and his Public Image*, London, 1972.

Yavez, T: *Augustus: The Victory of Moderation* (in Hebrew), Tel Aviv, 1988.

On line Bibliography

www.math.ucsd.edu

www.Armas y Ritos de la Iberia Preromana

www.uoregon.edu/kilo/maps/rr/general/B270MED

www.principialegionis.orgfilesRoman_Army_Fo]

http://myweb.unomaha.edu/~mreames/Alexander/sarissa_jones.html

scottthong.files.wordpress.com/2007/05/

Index